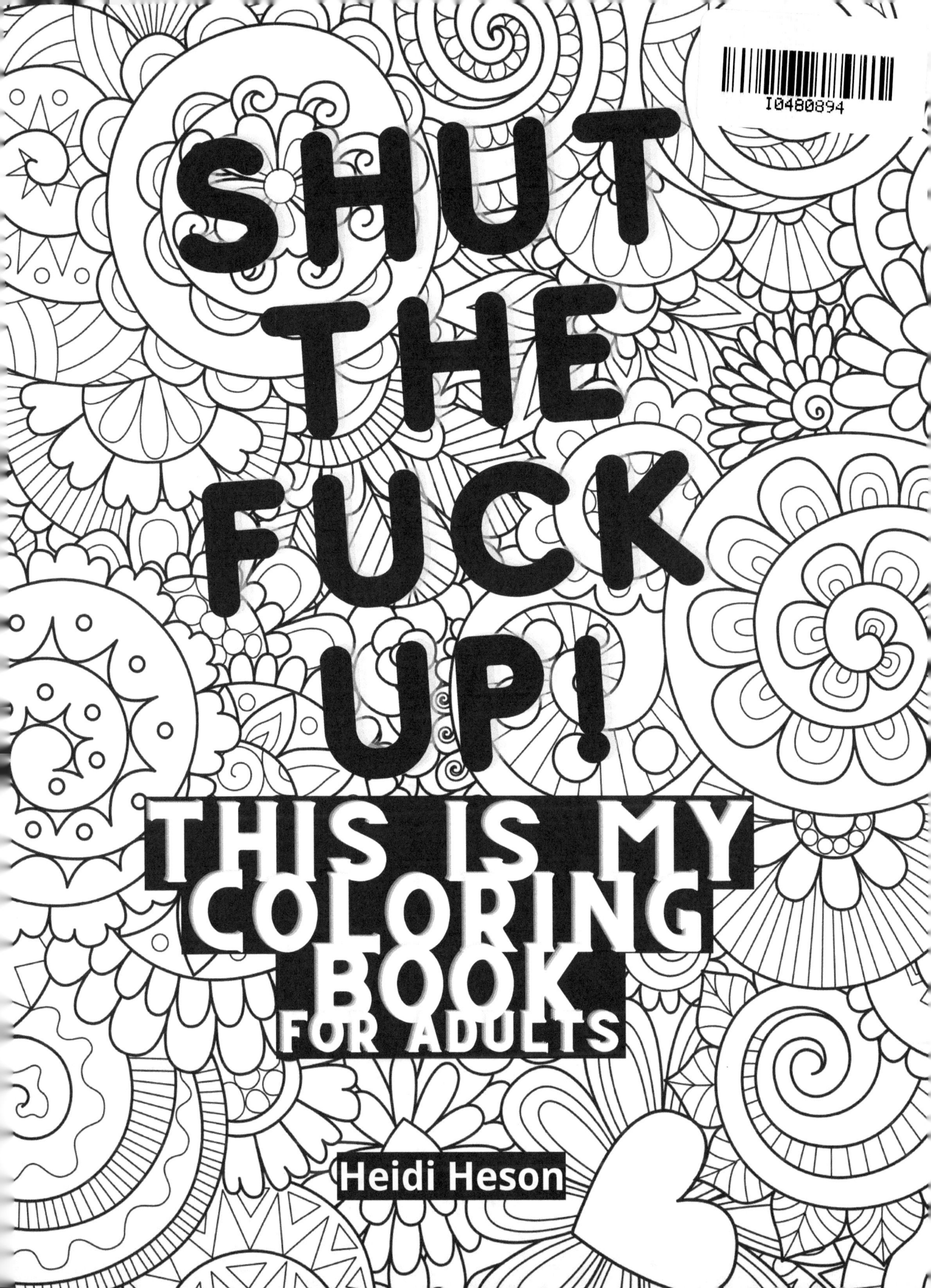

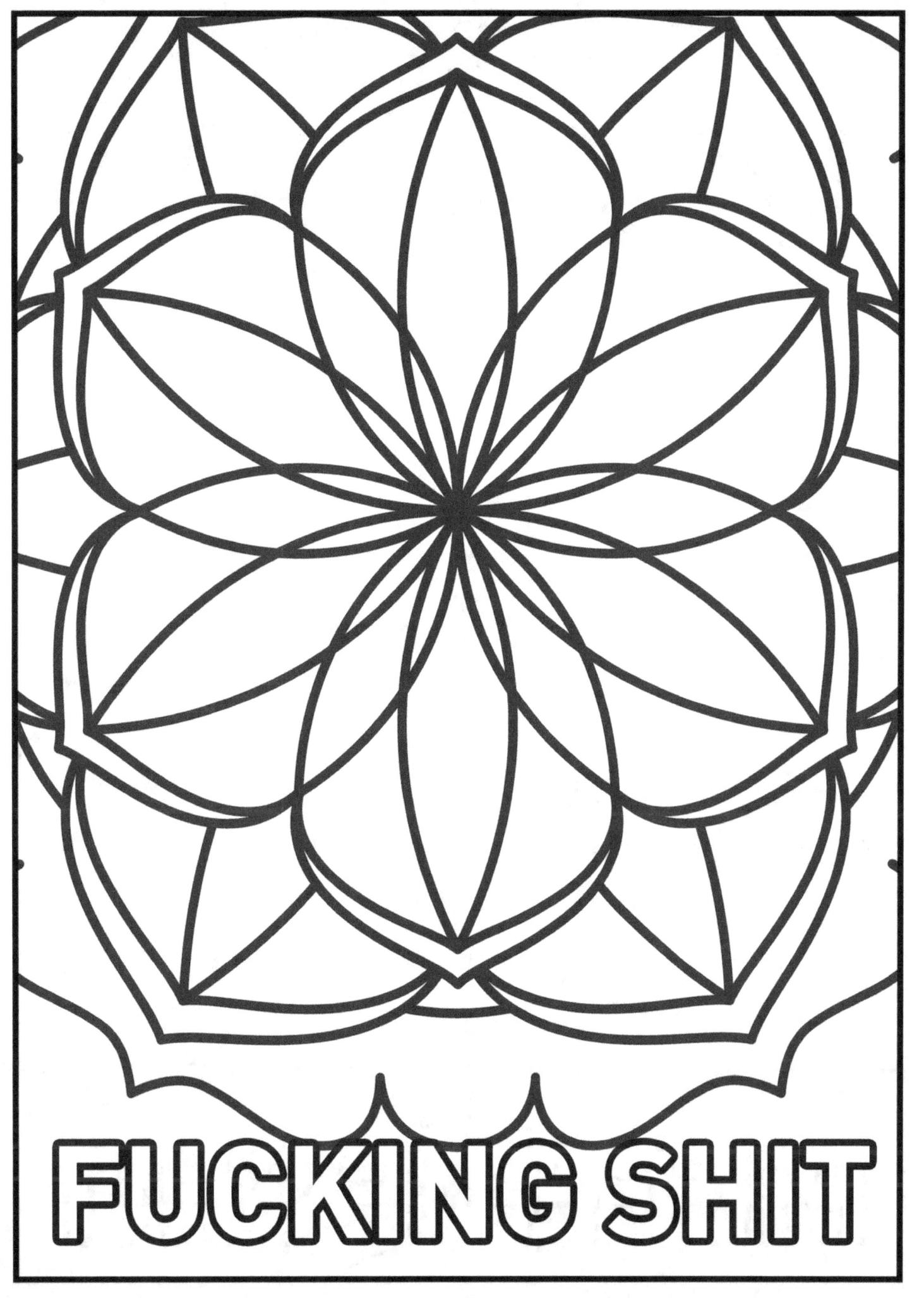

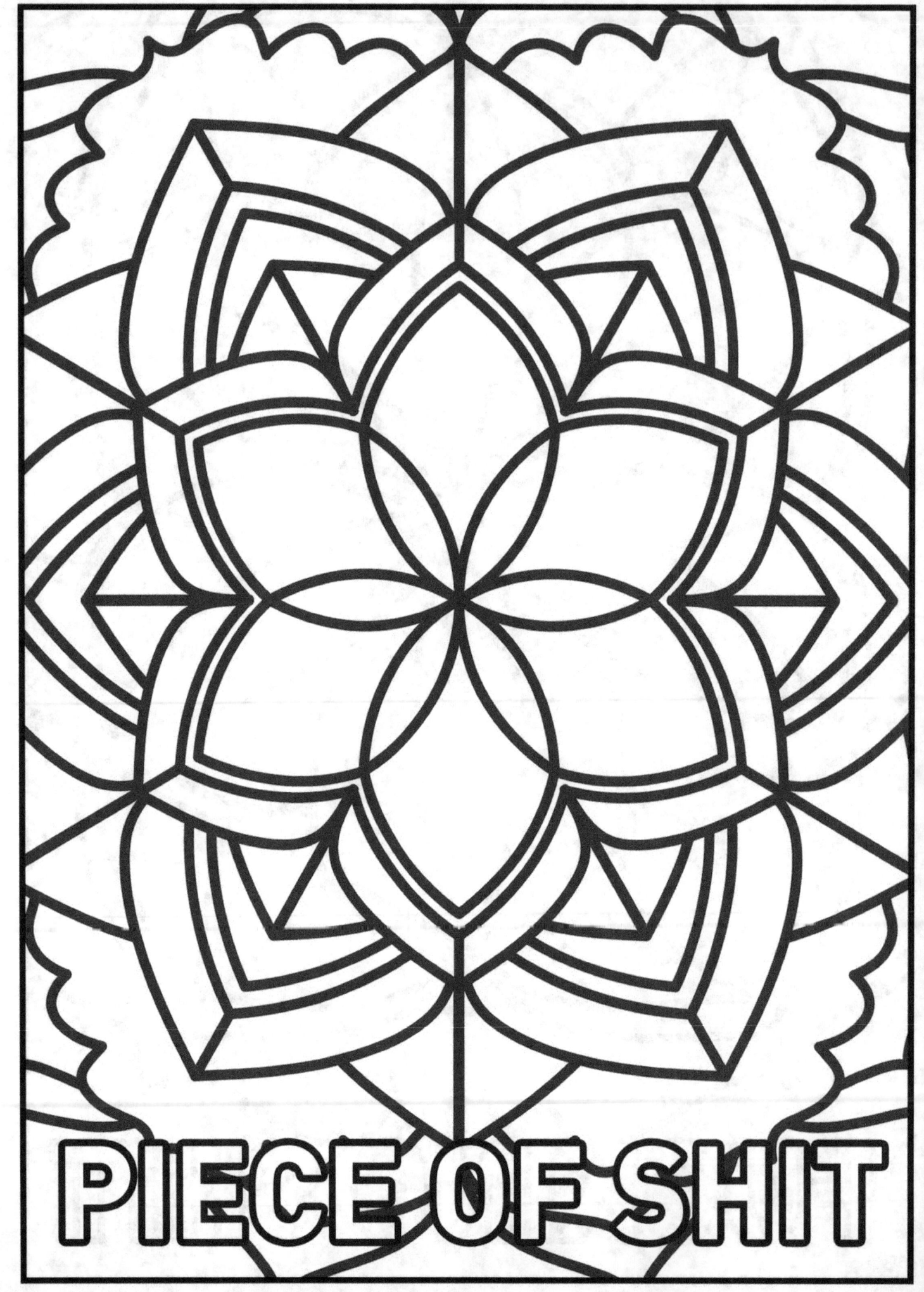

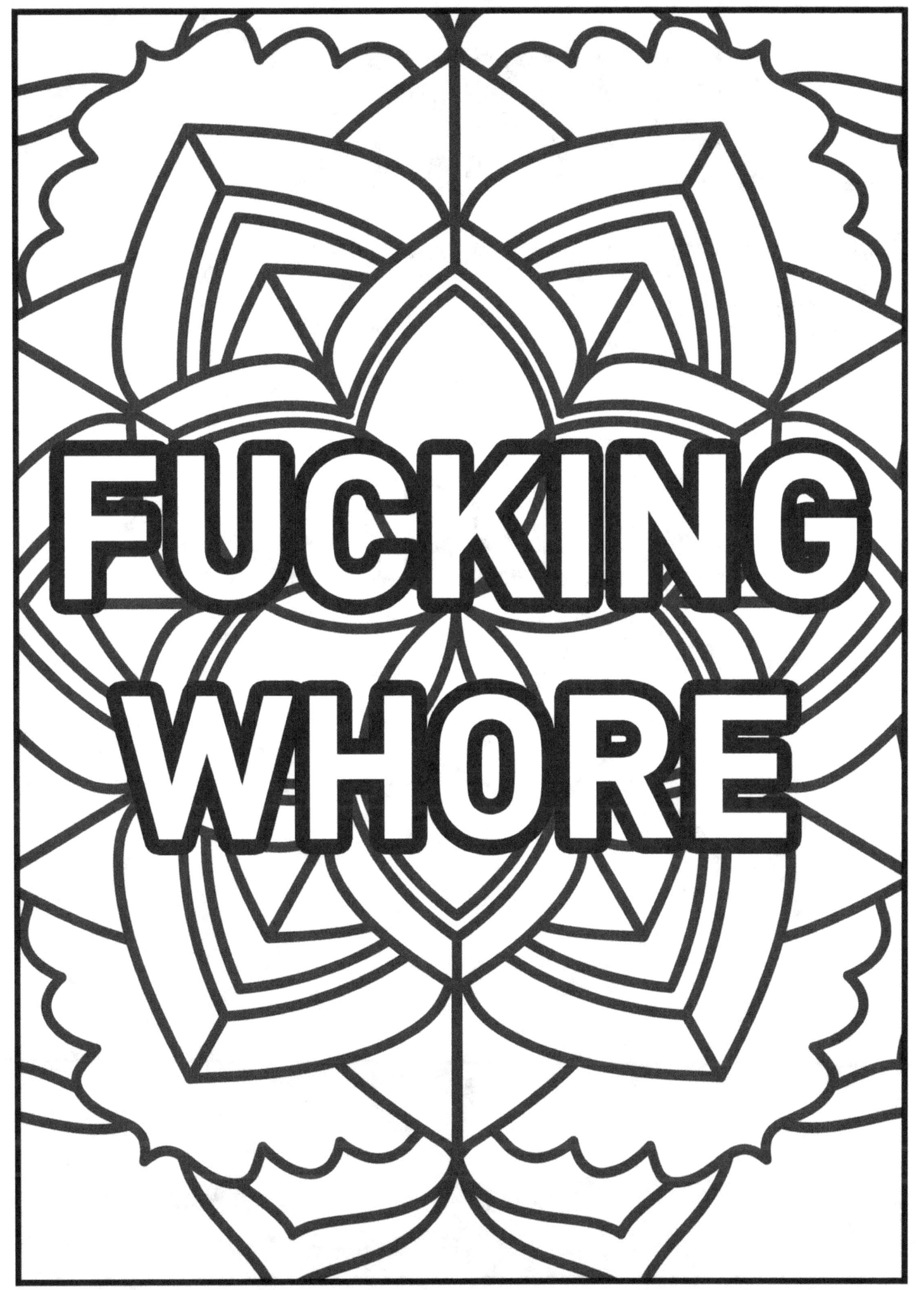

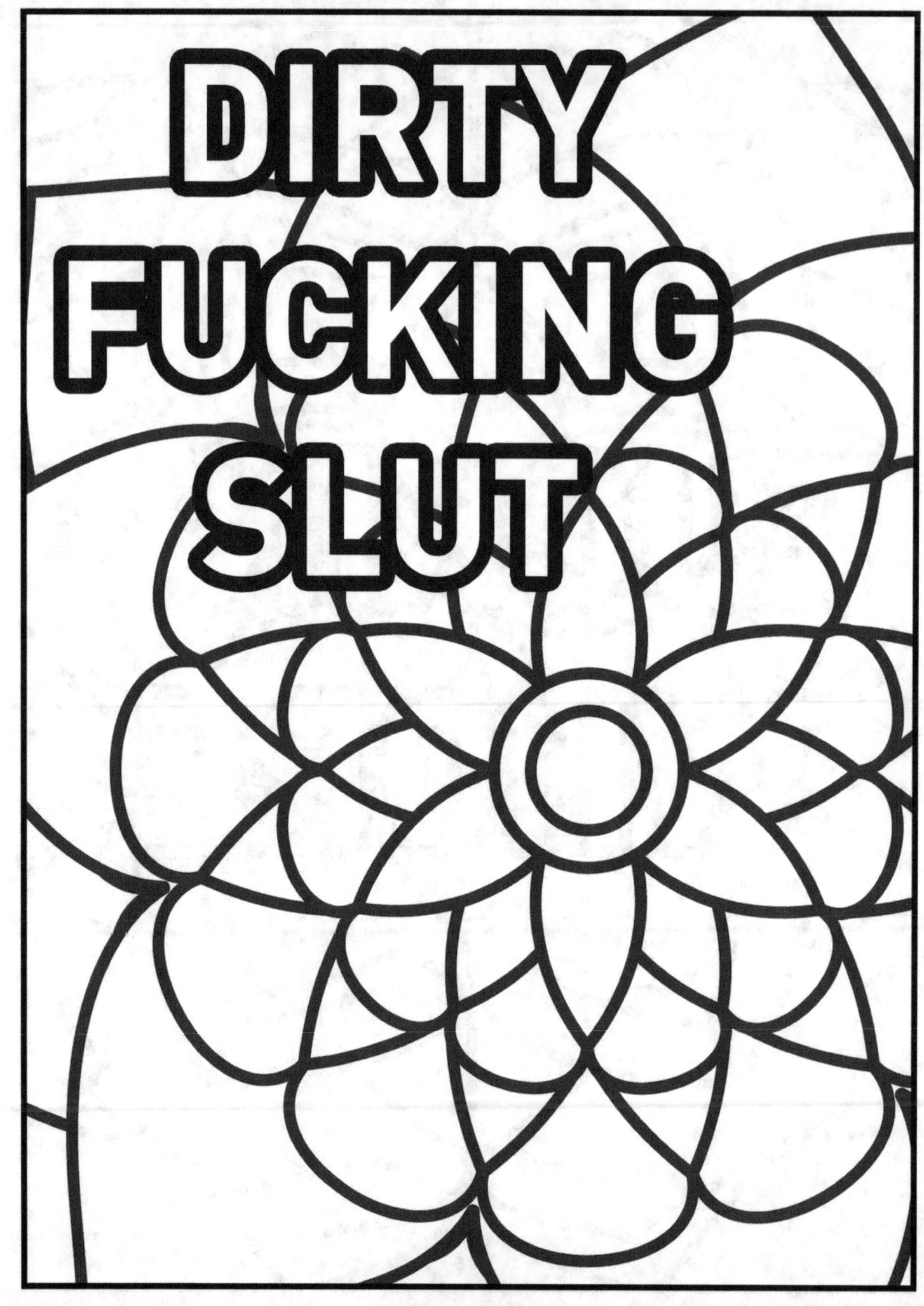

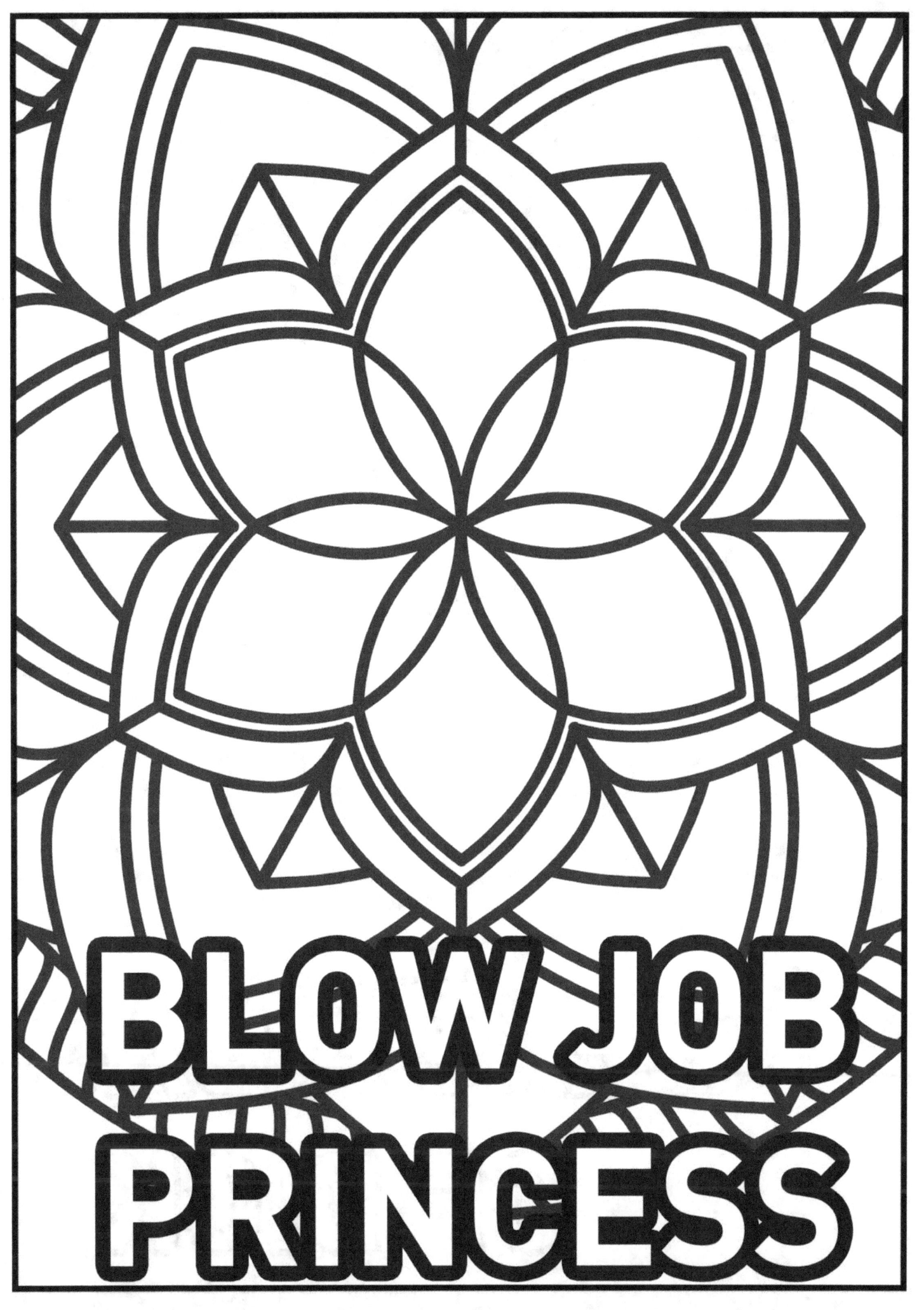

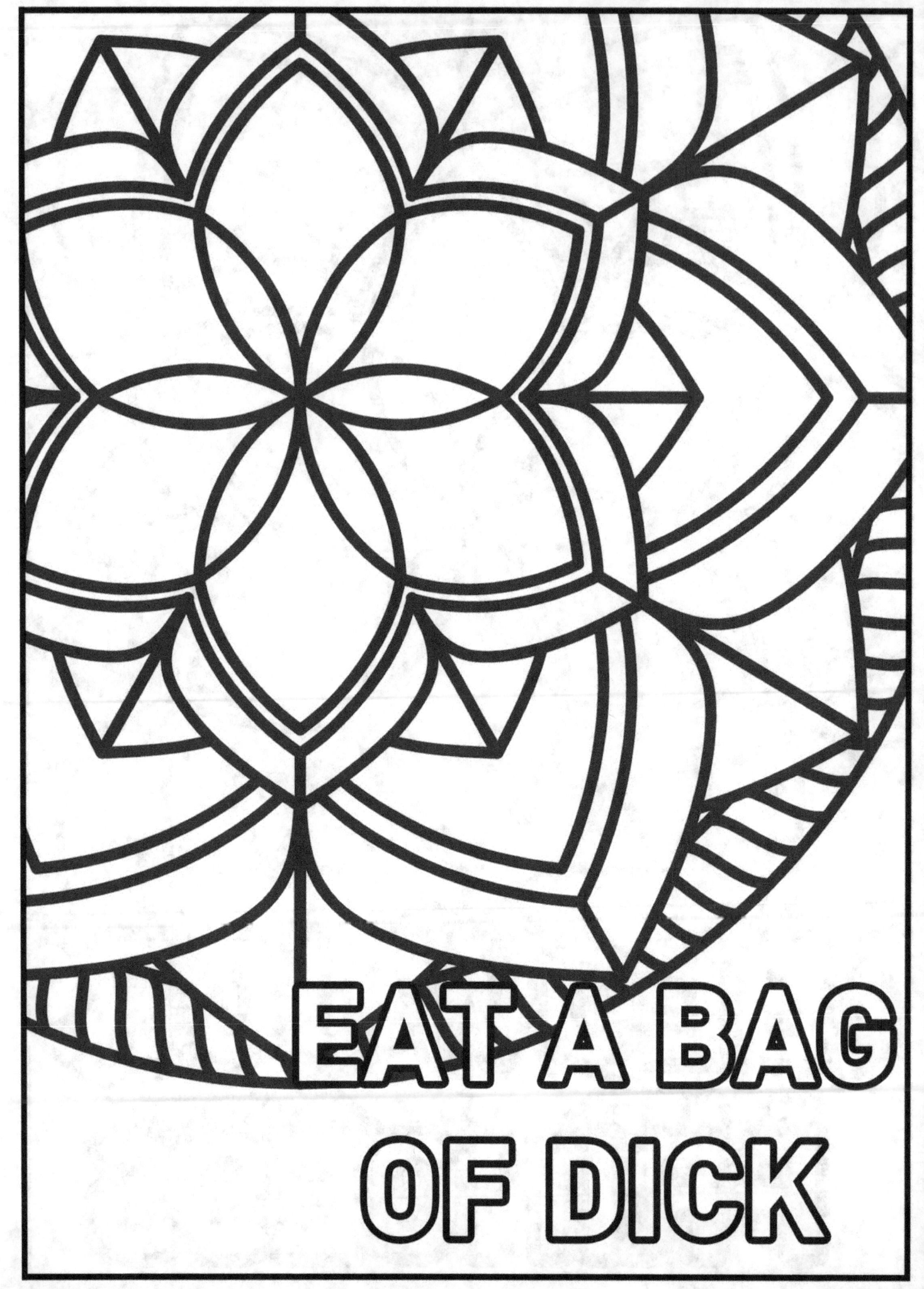

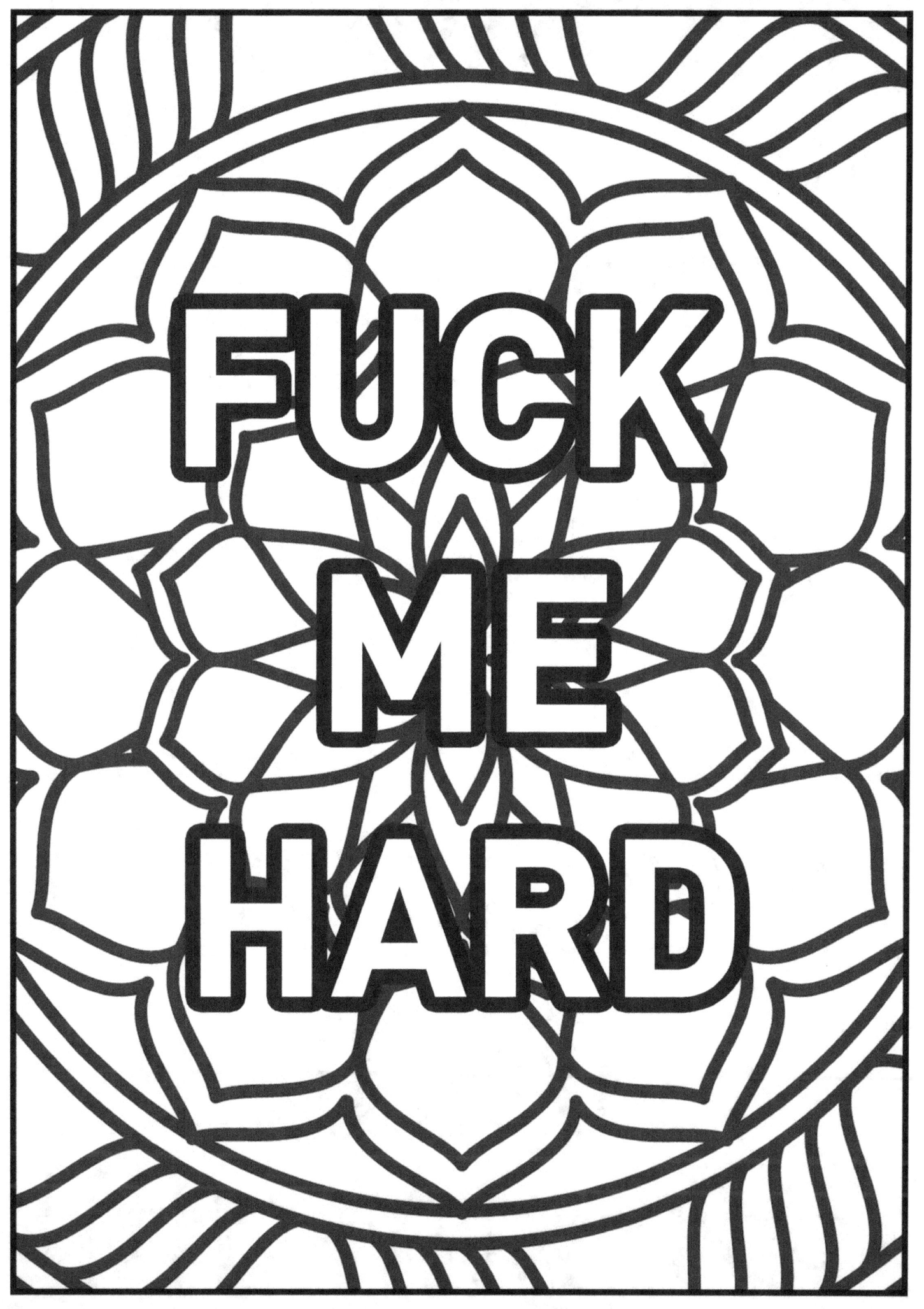

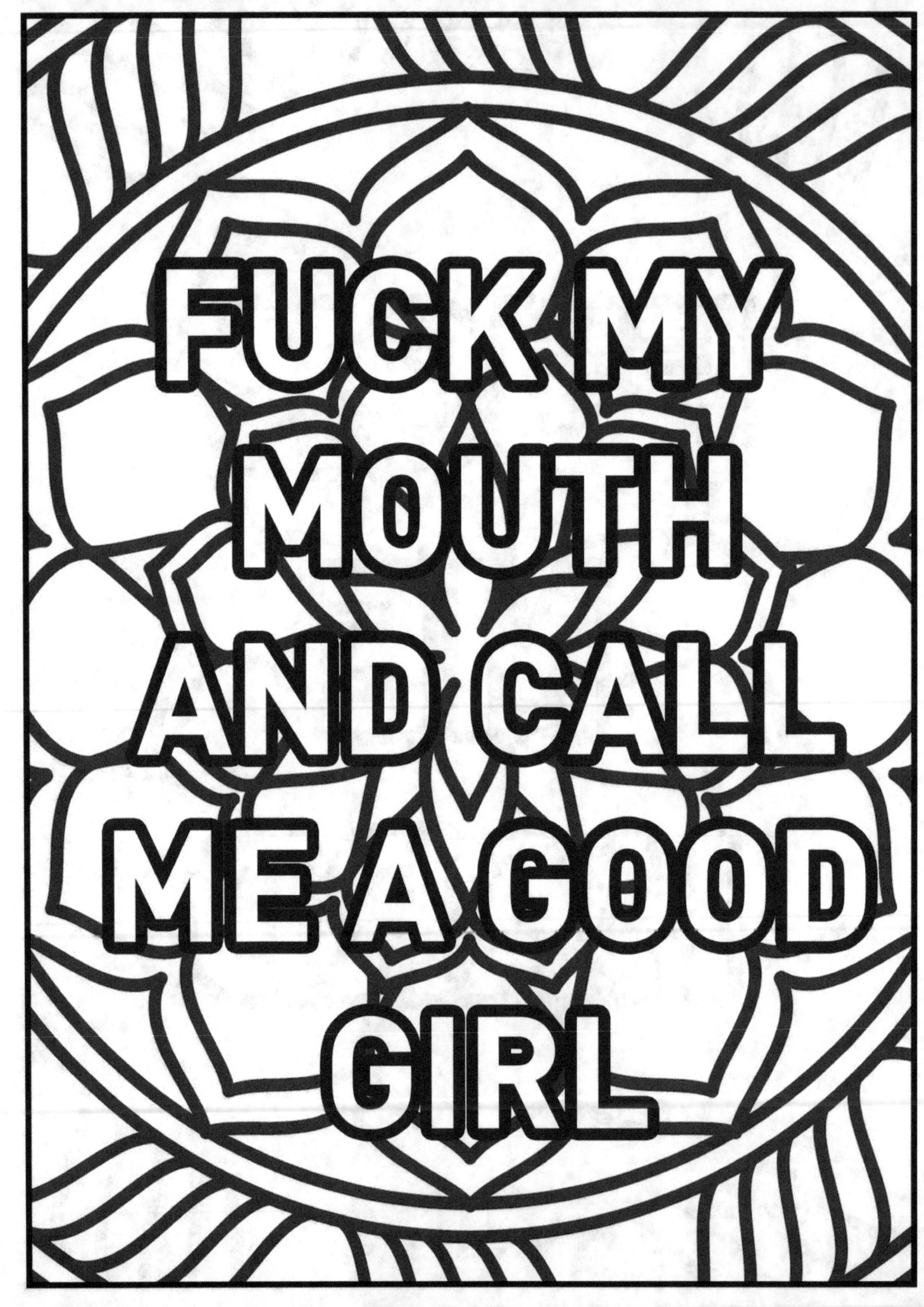

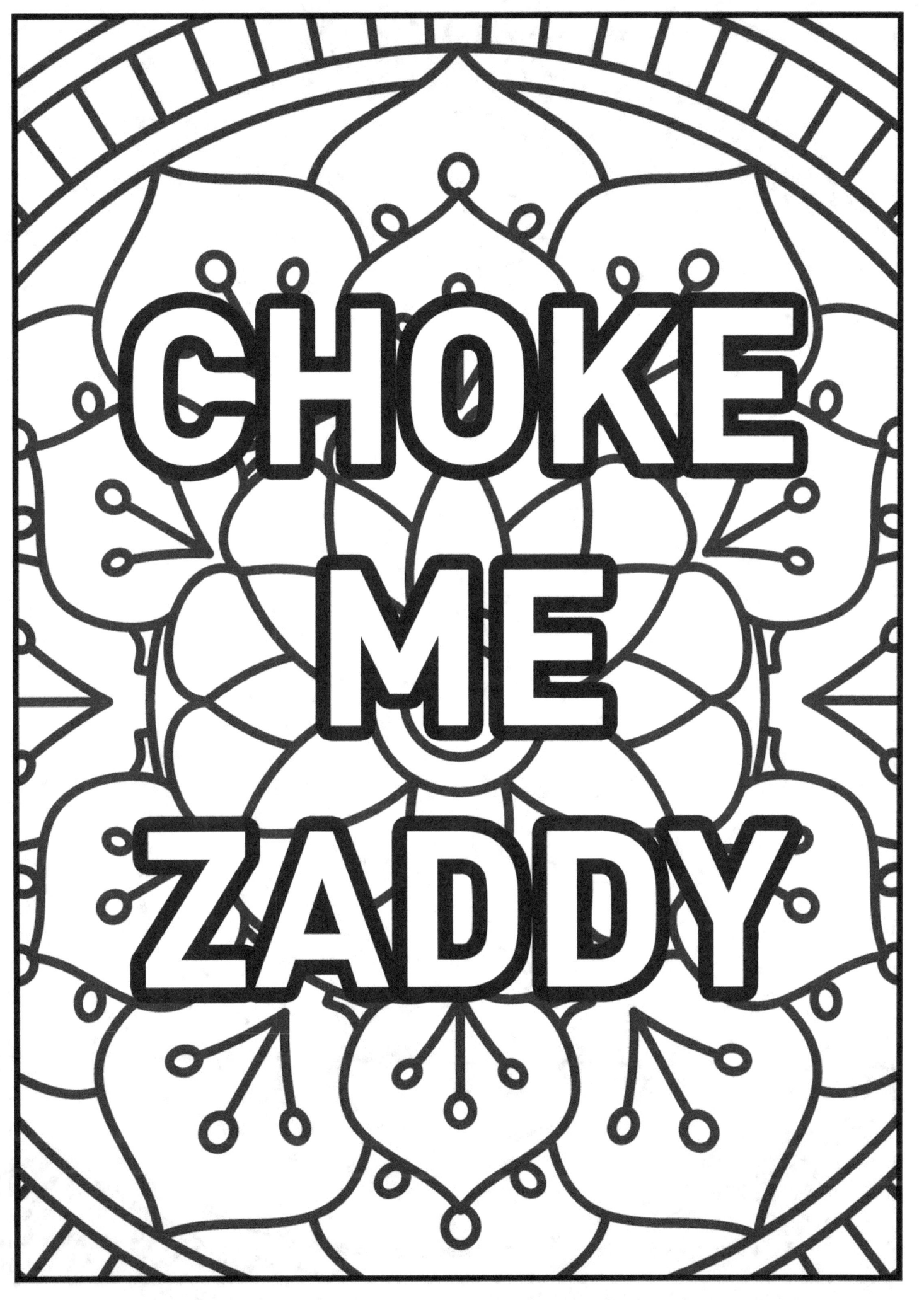

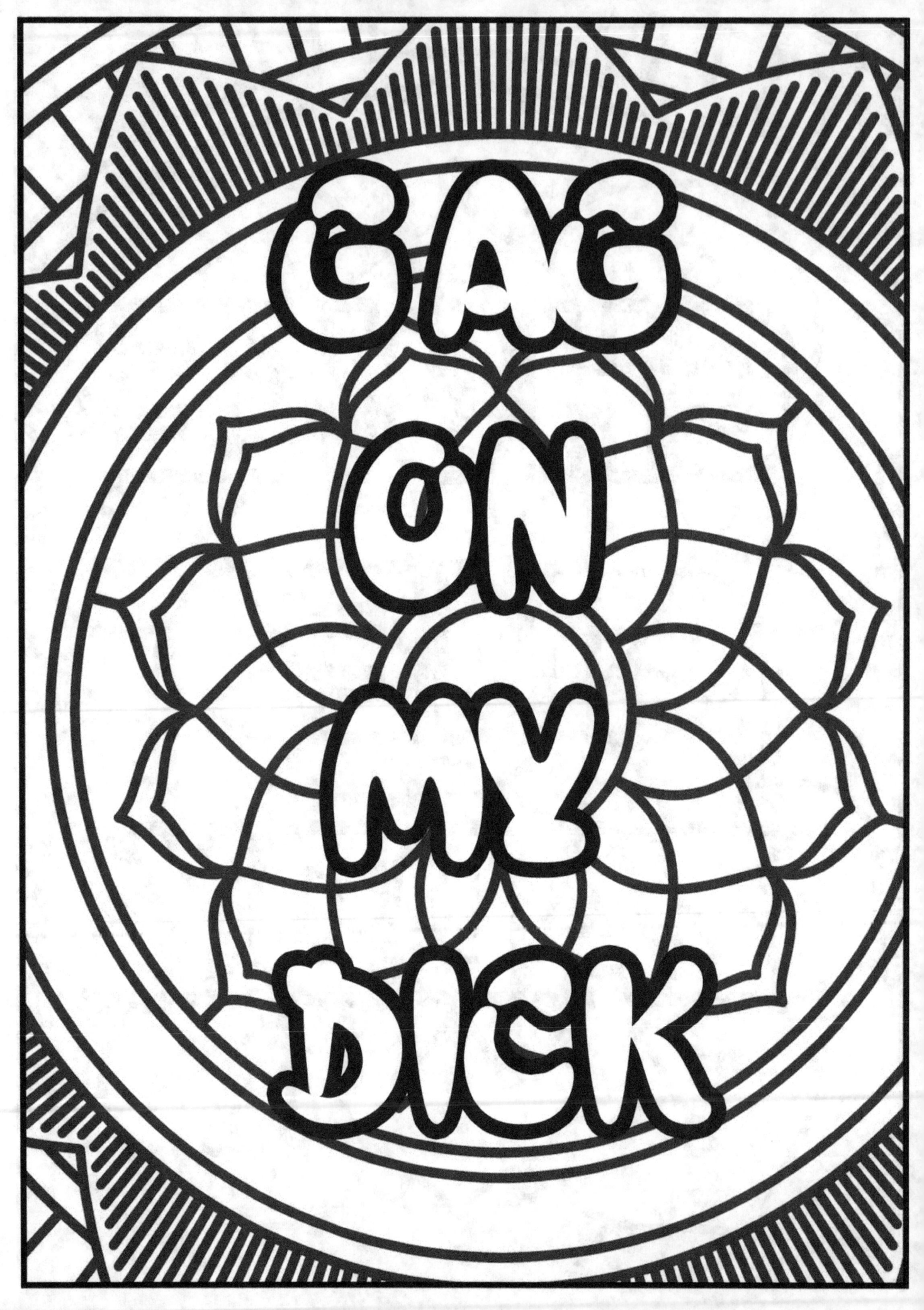

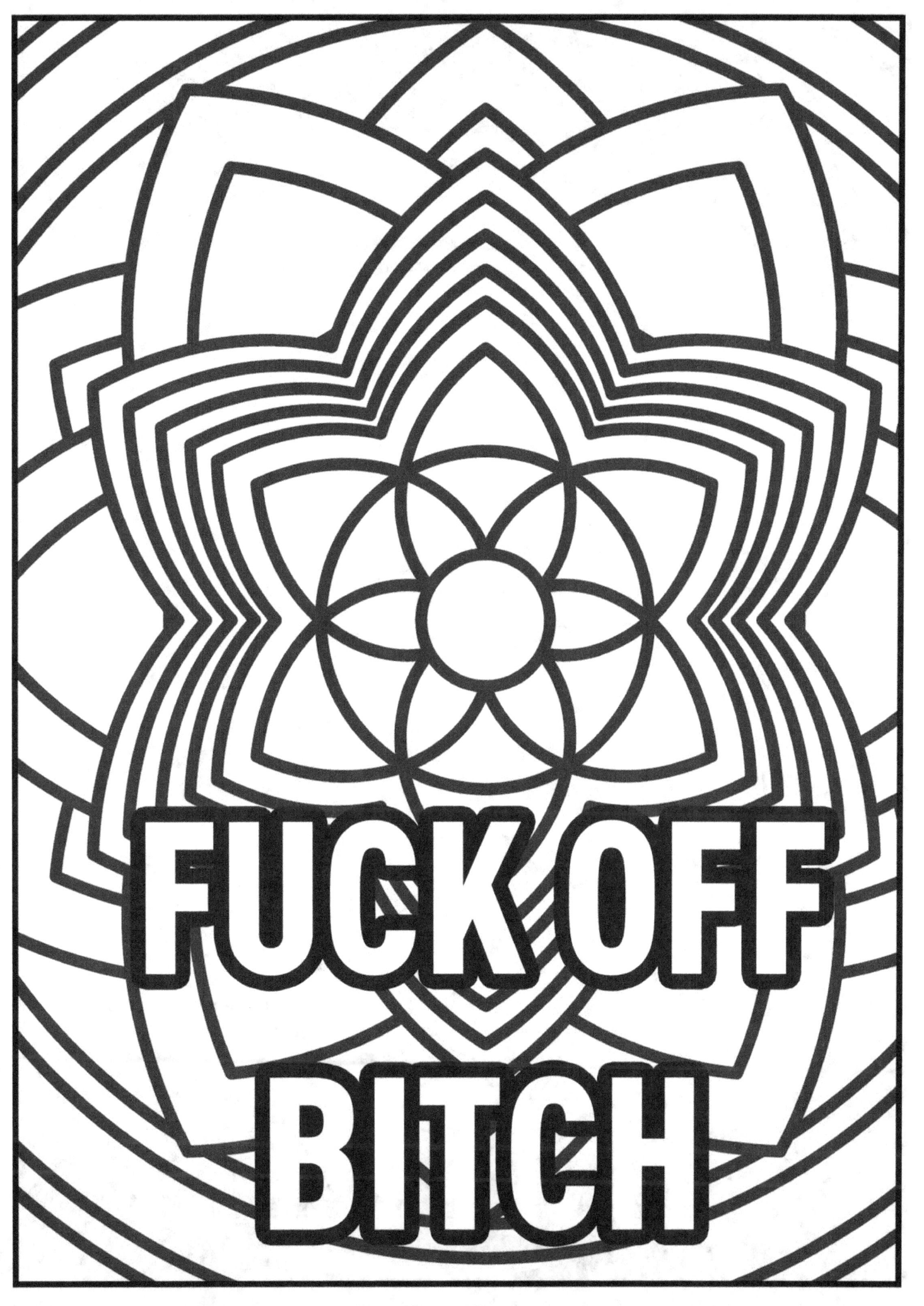

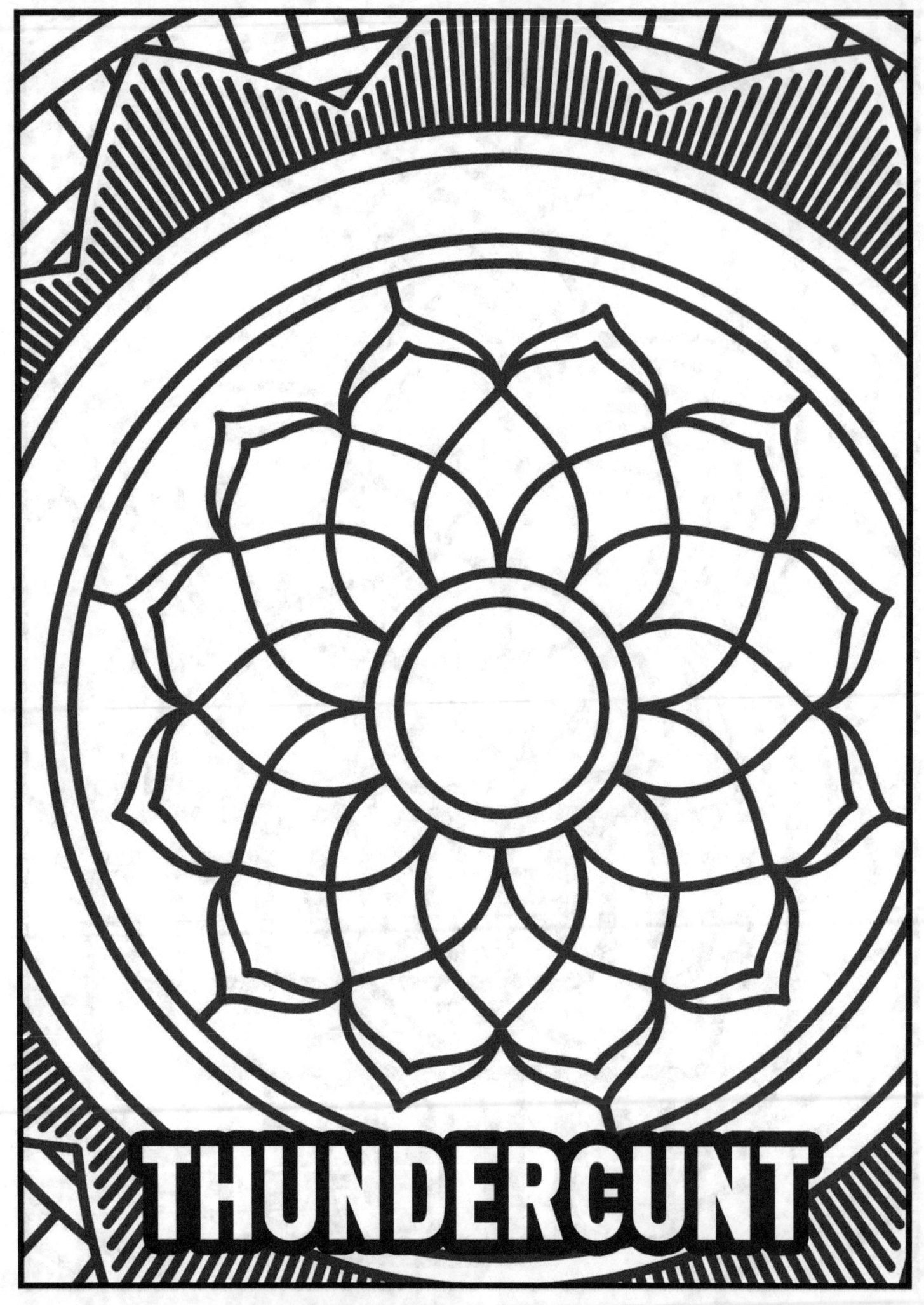

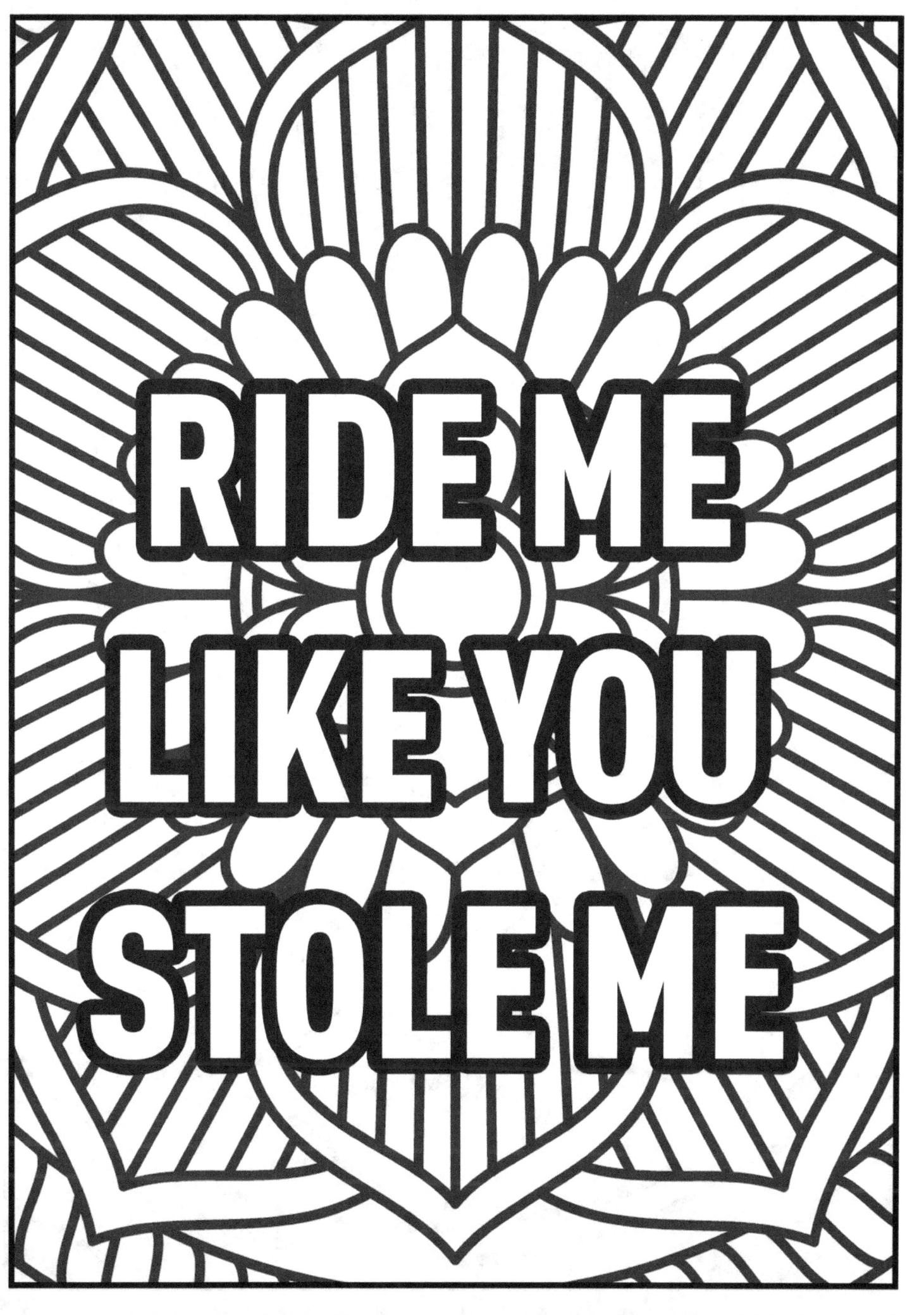

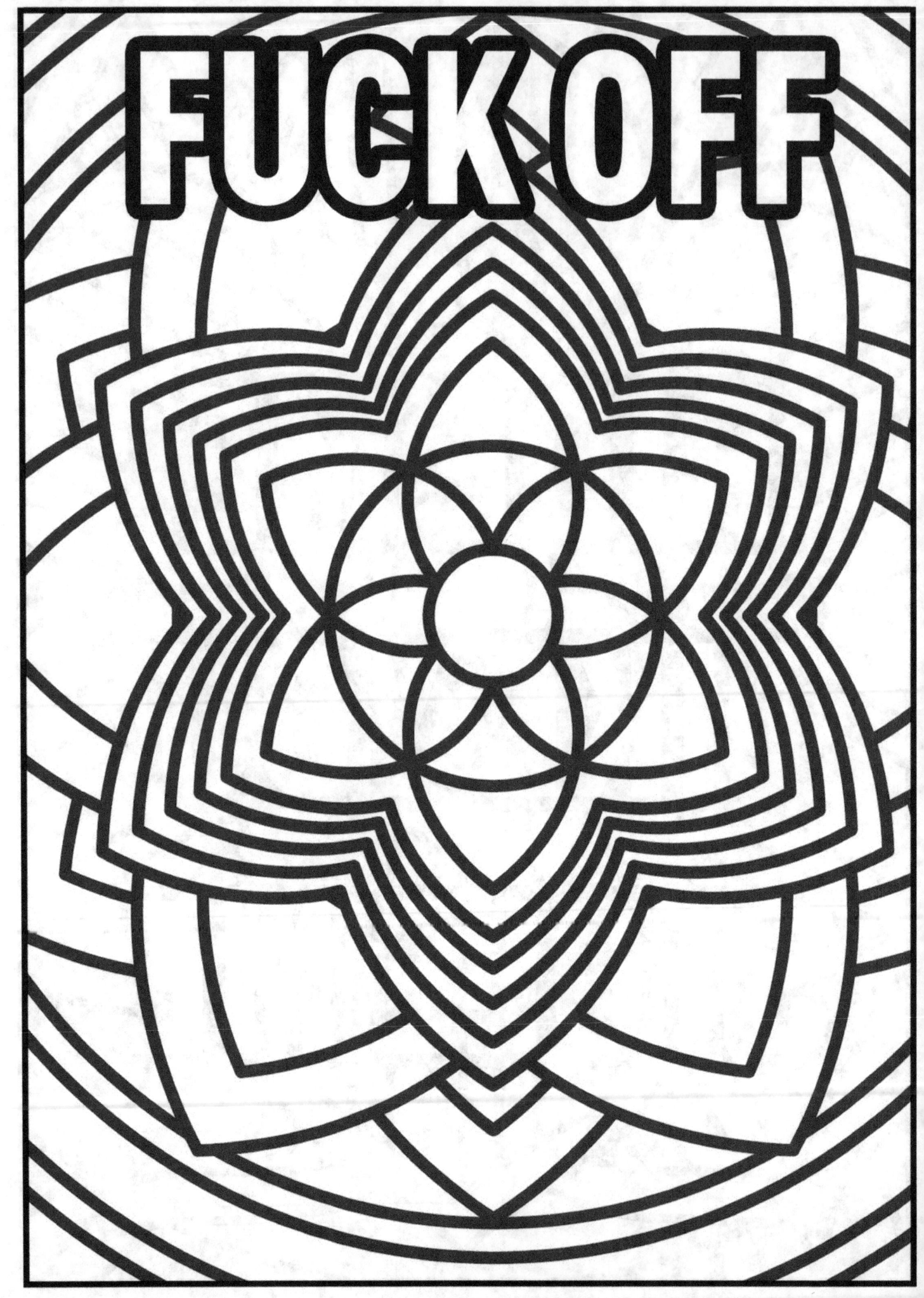

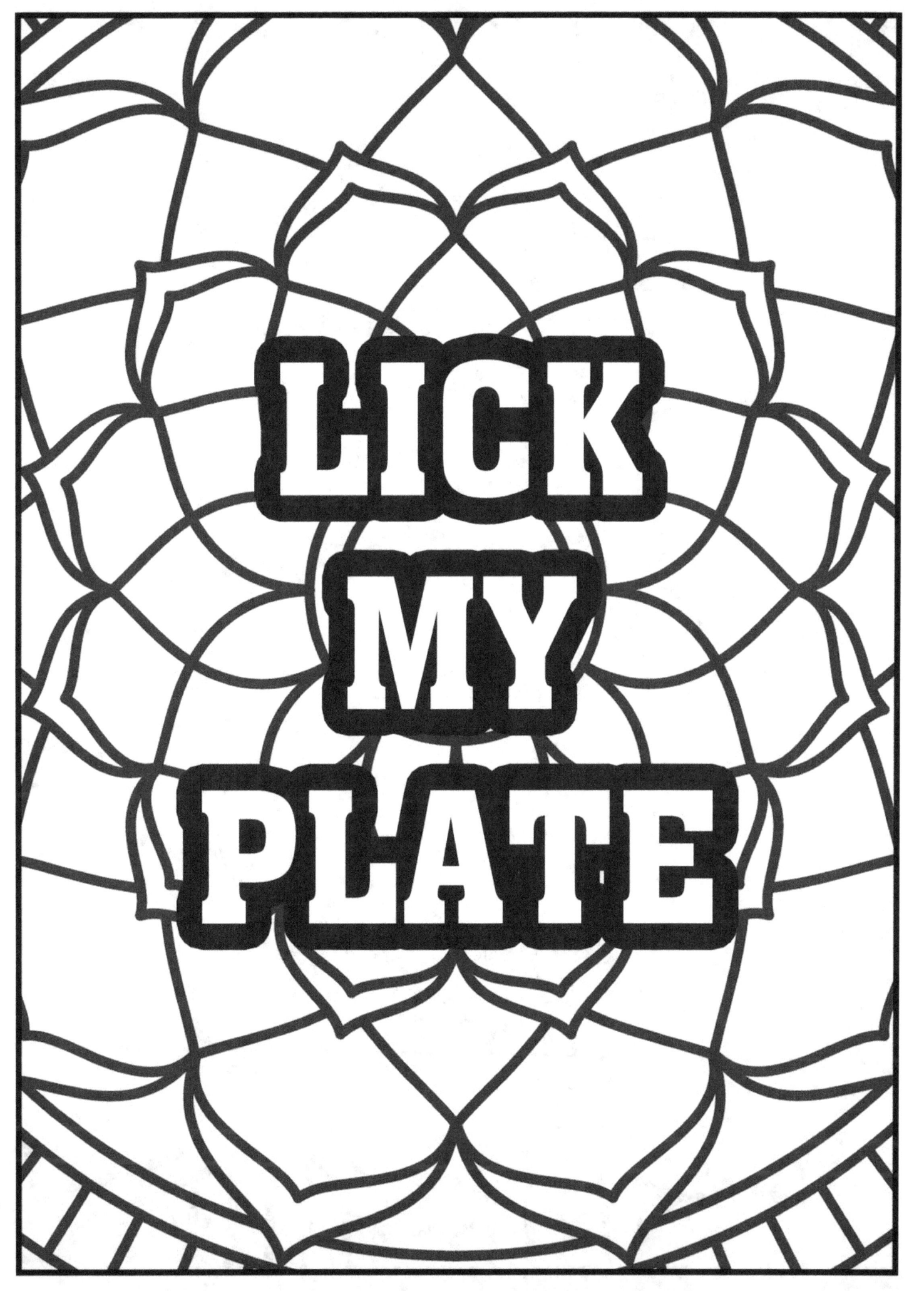

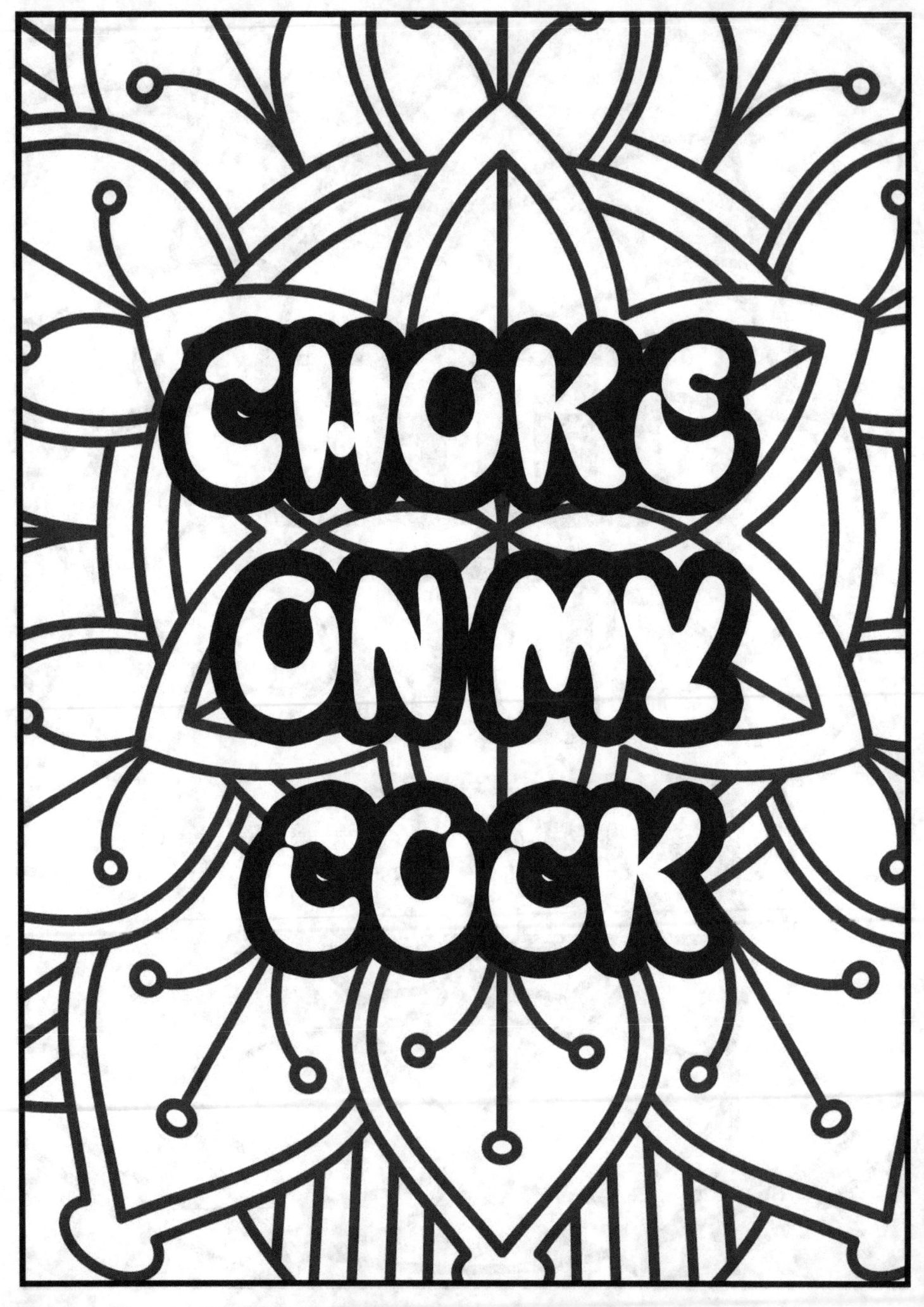

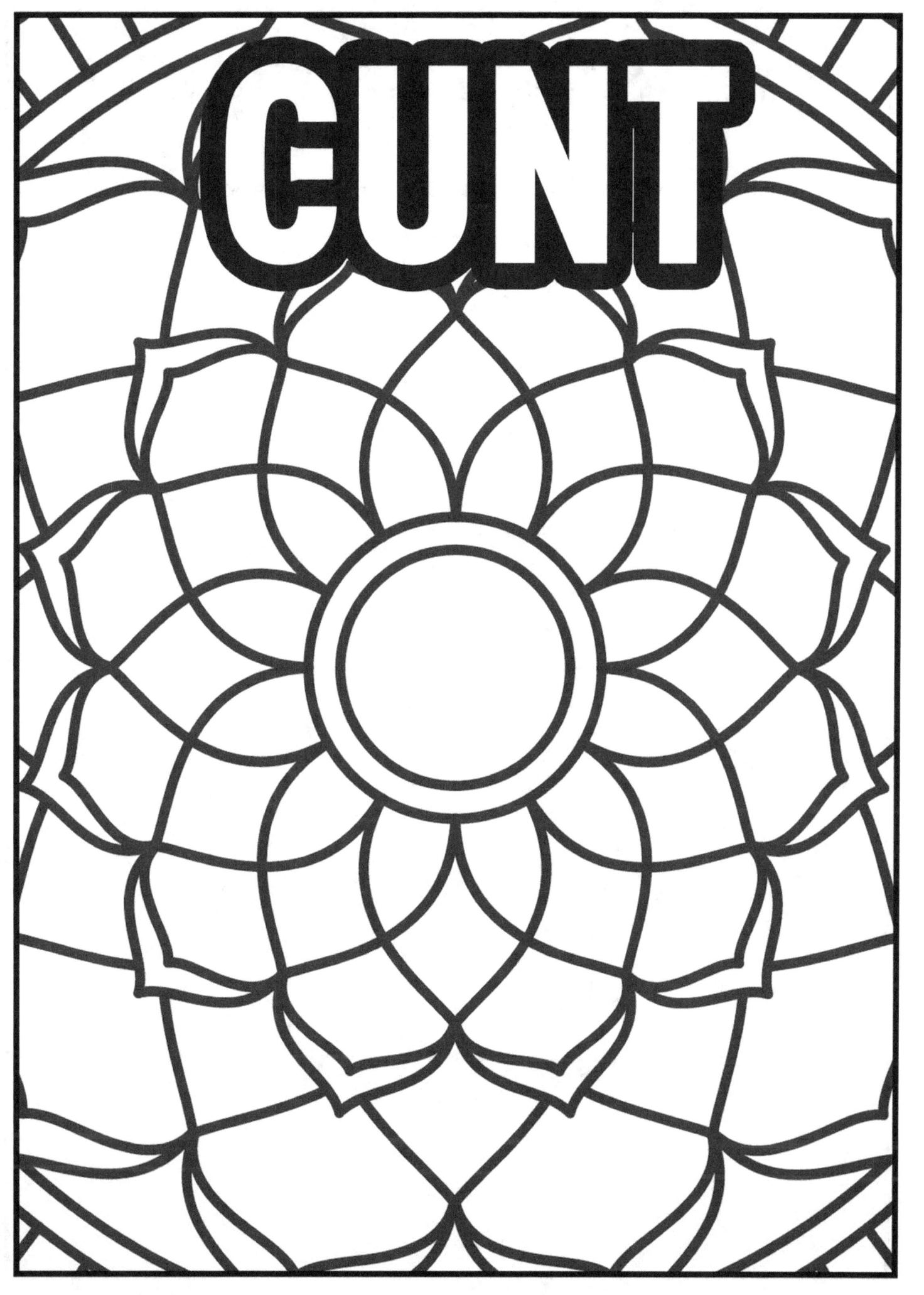

VAGITARIAN

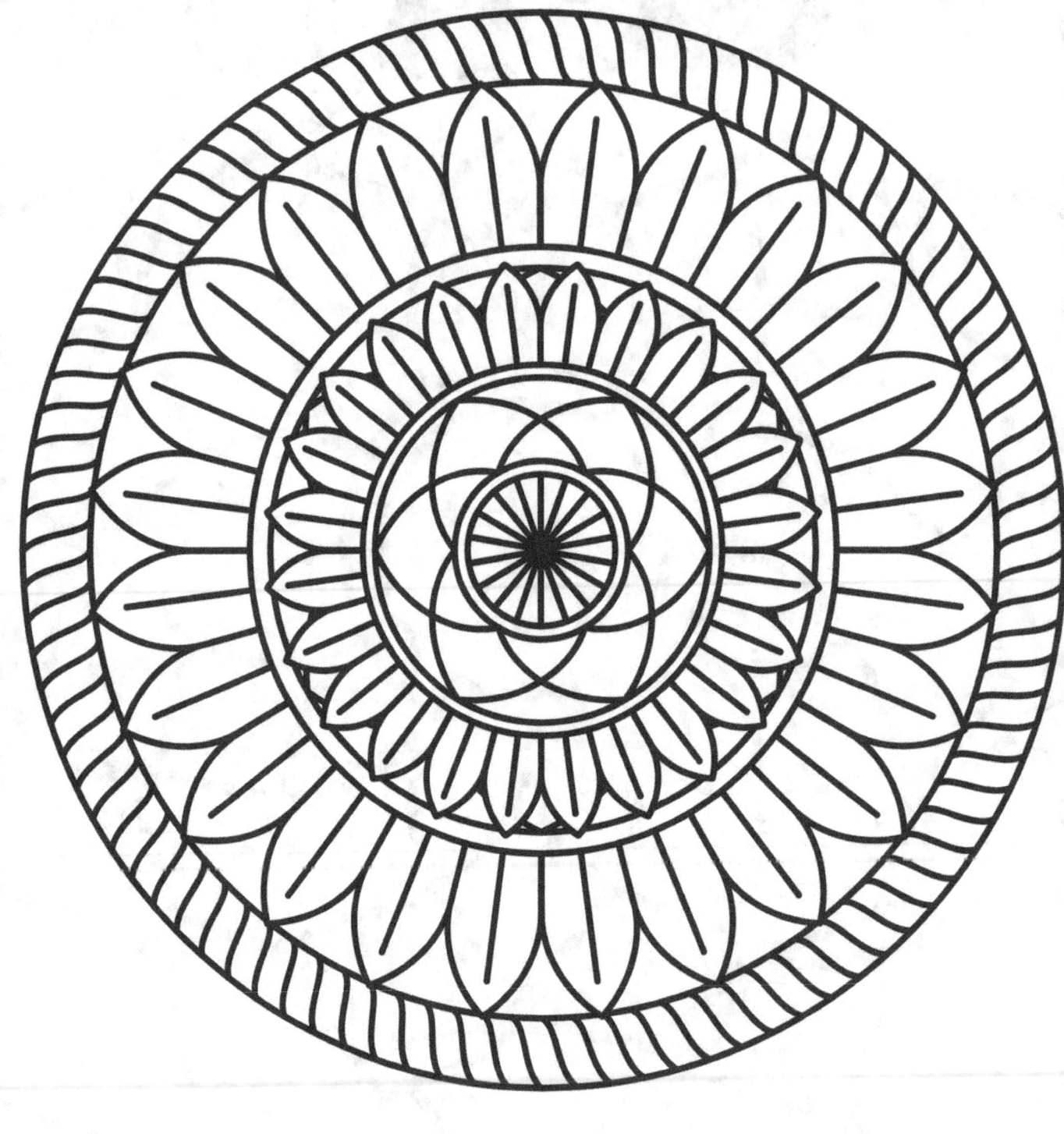

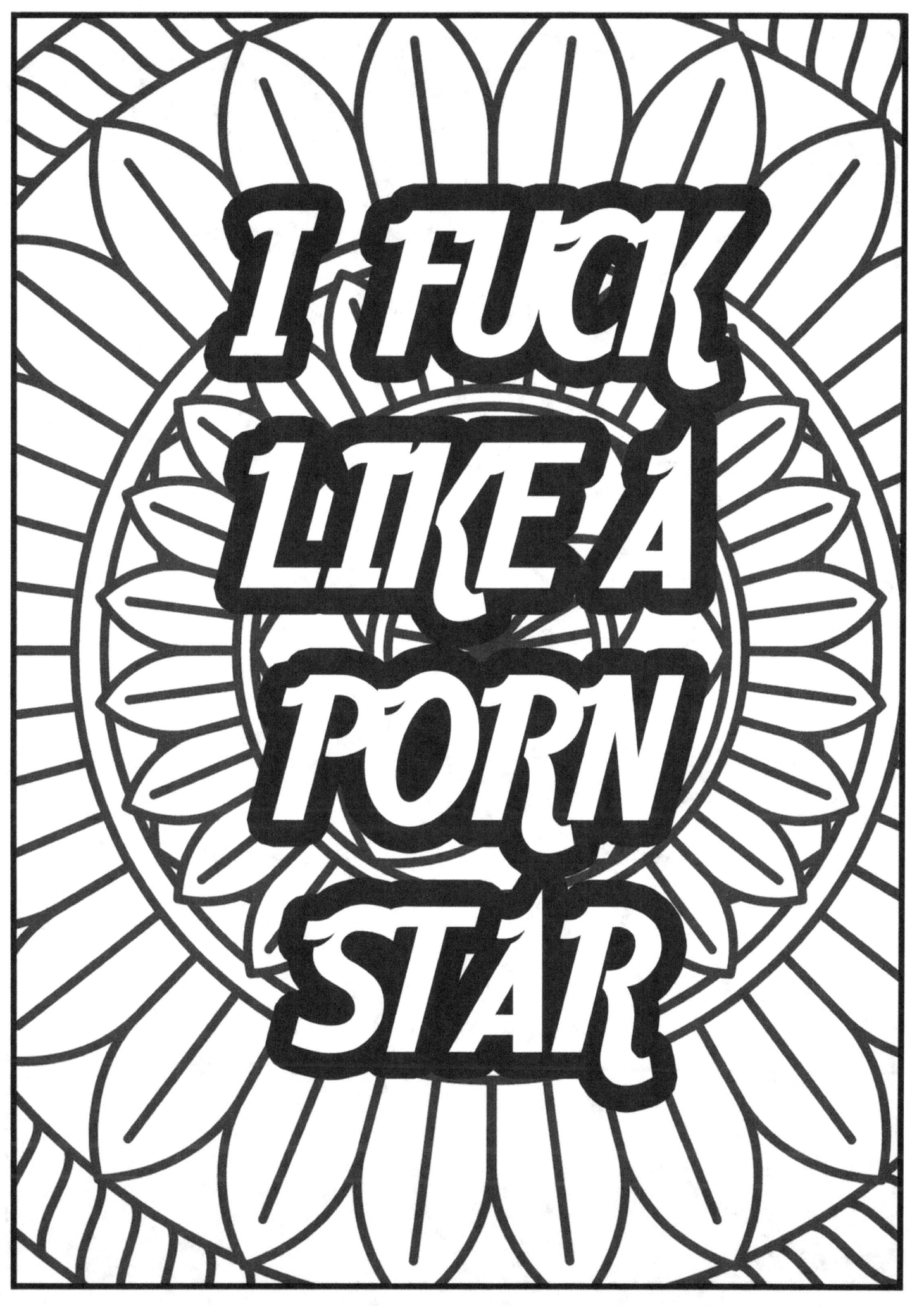

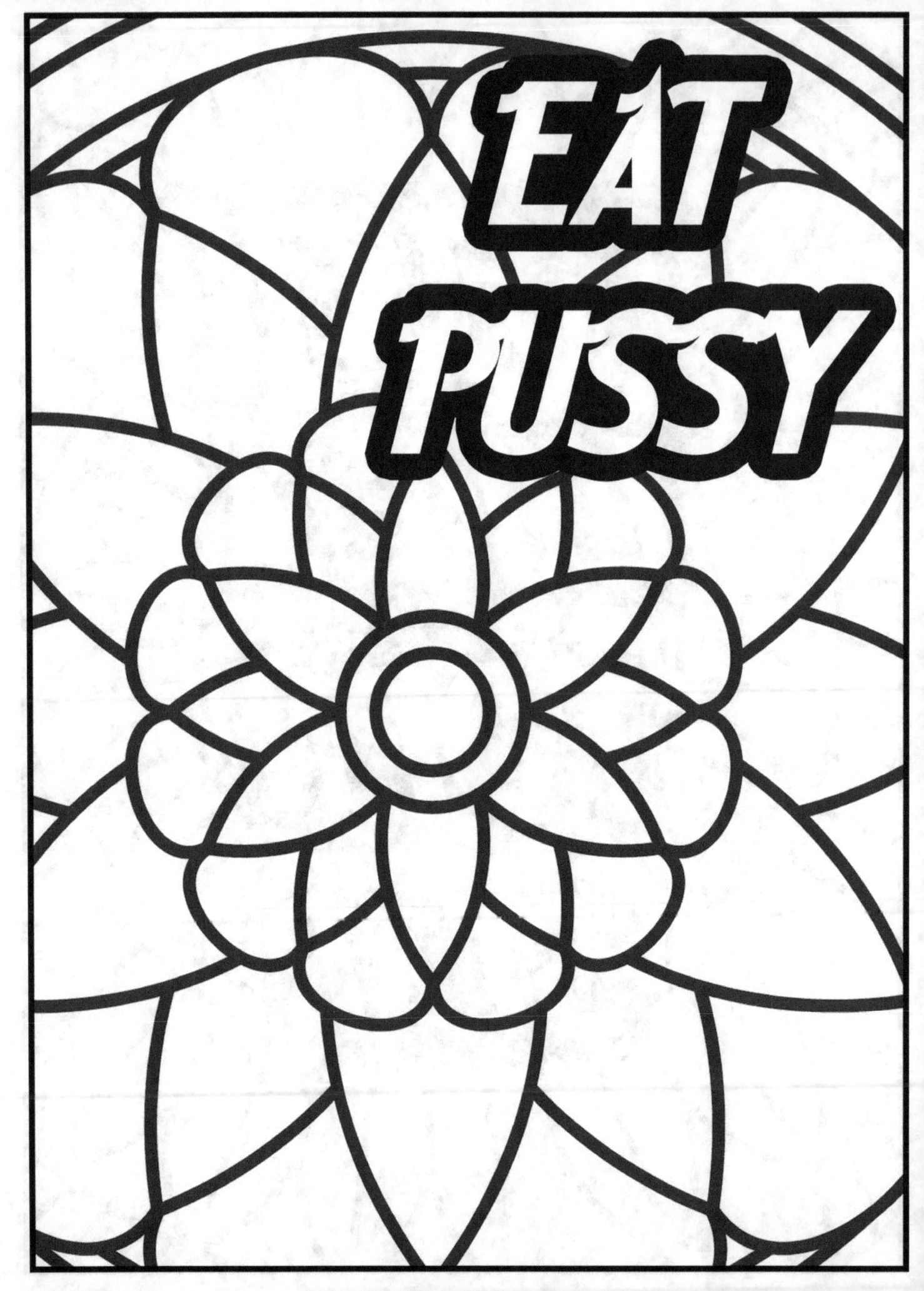

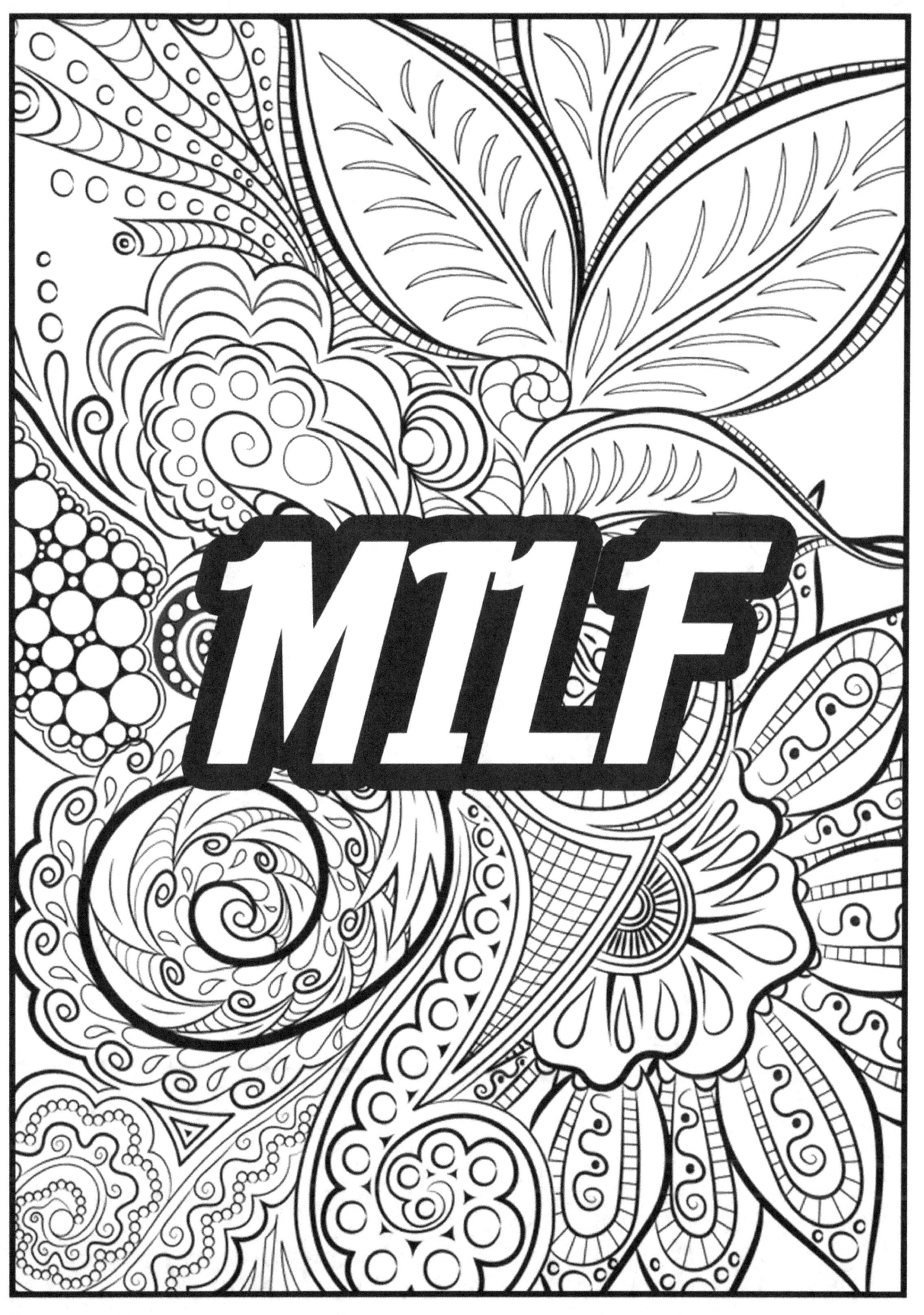

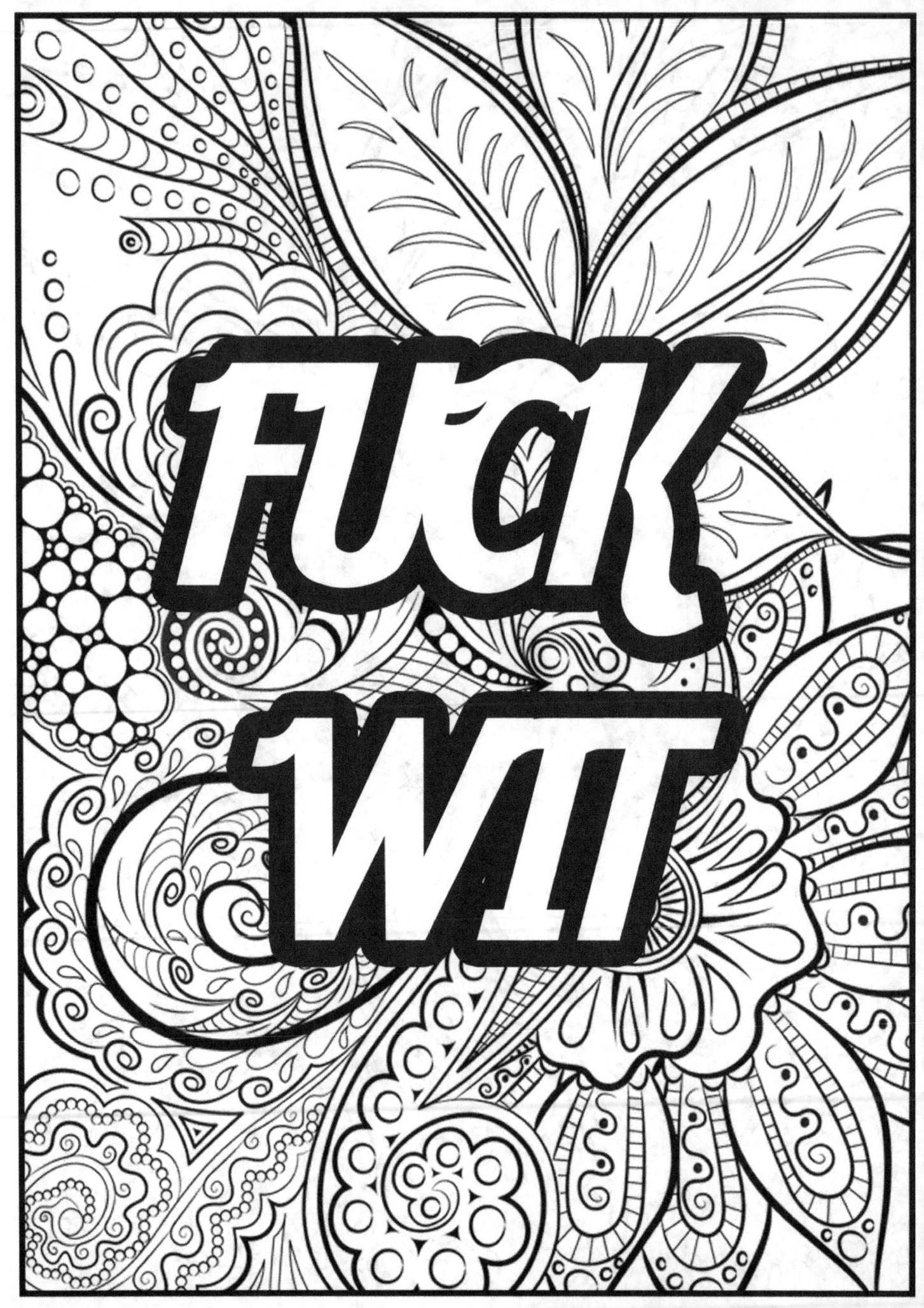

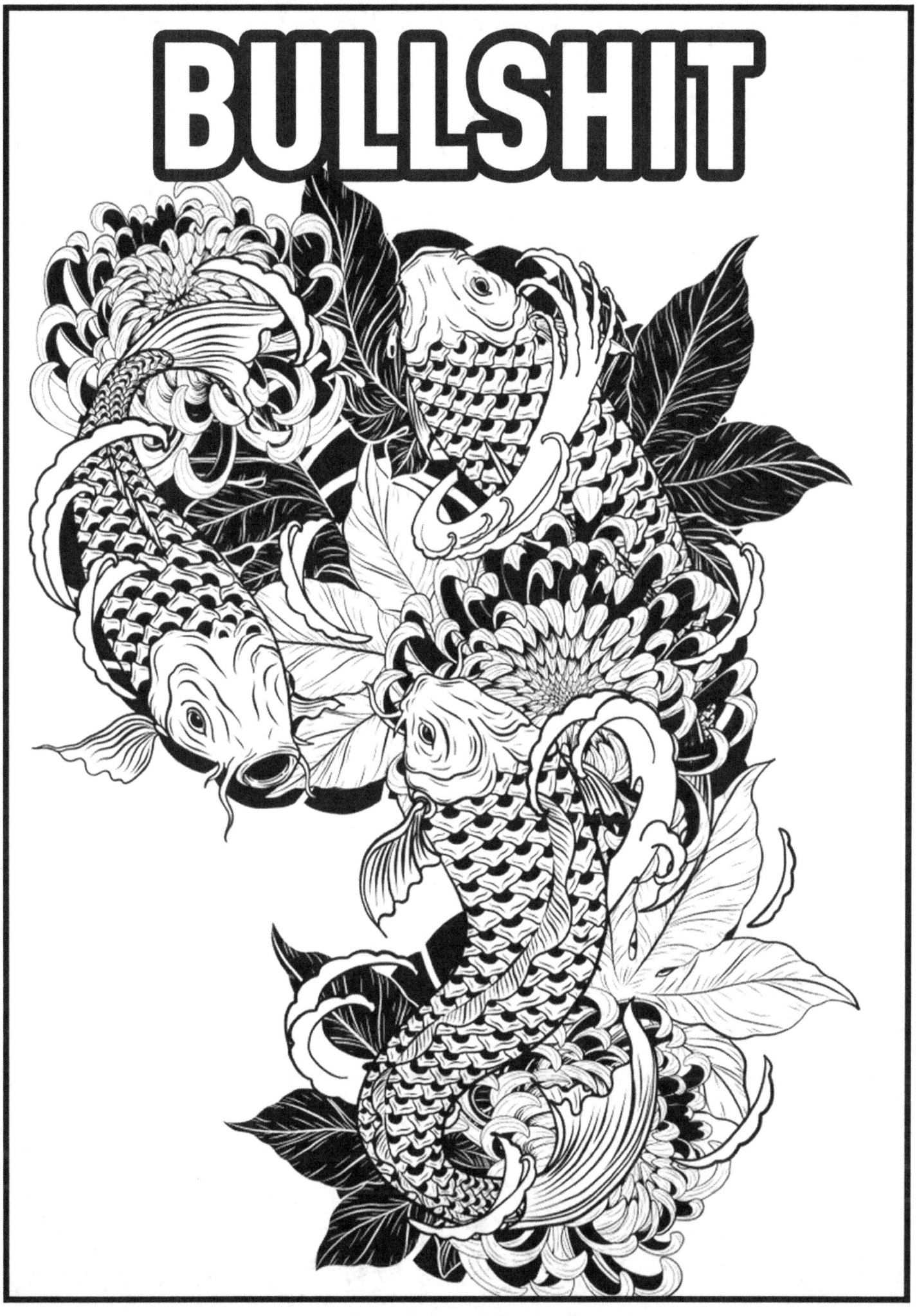

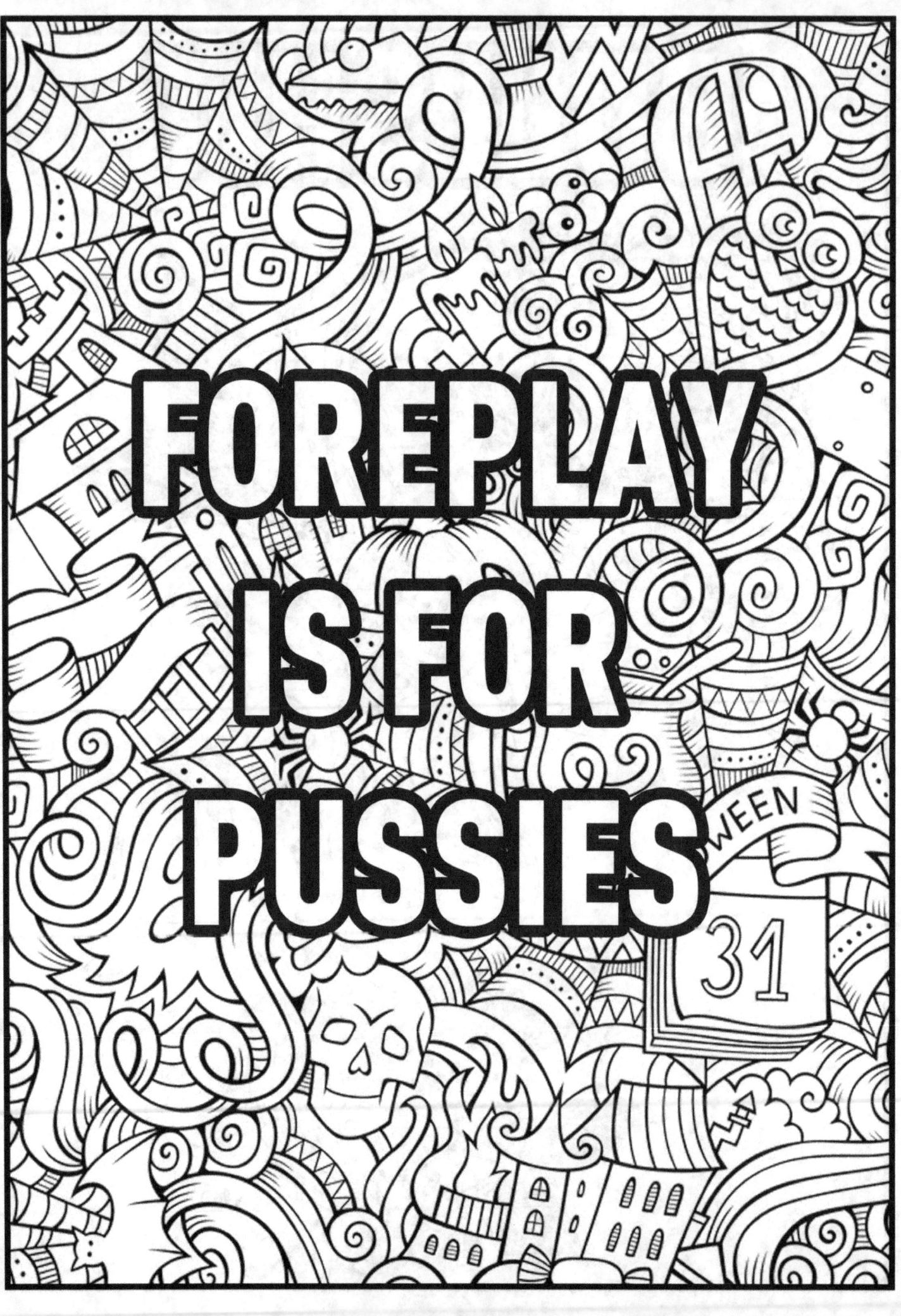

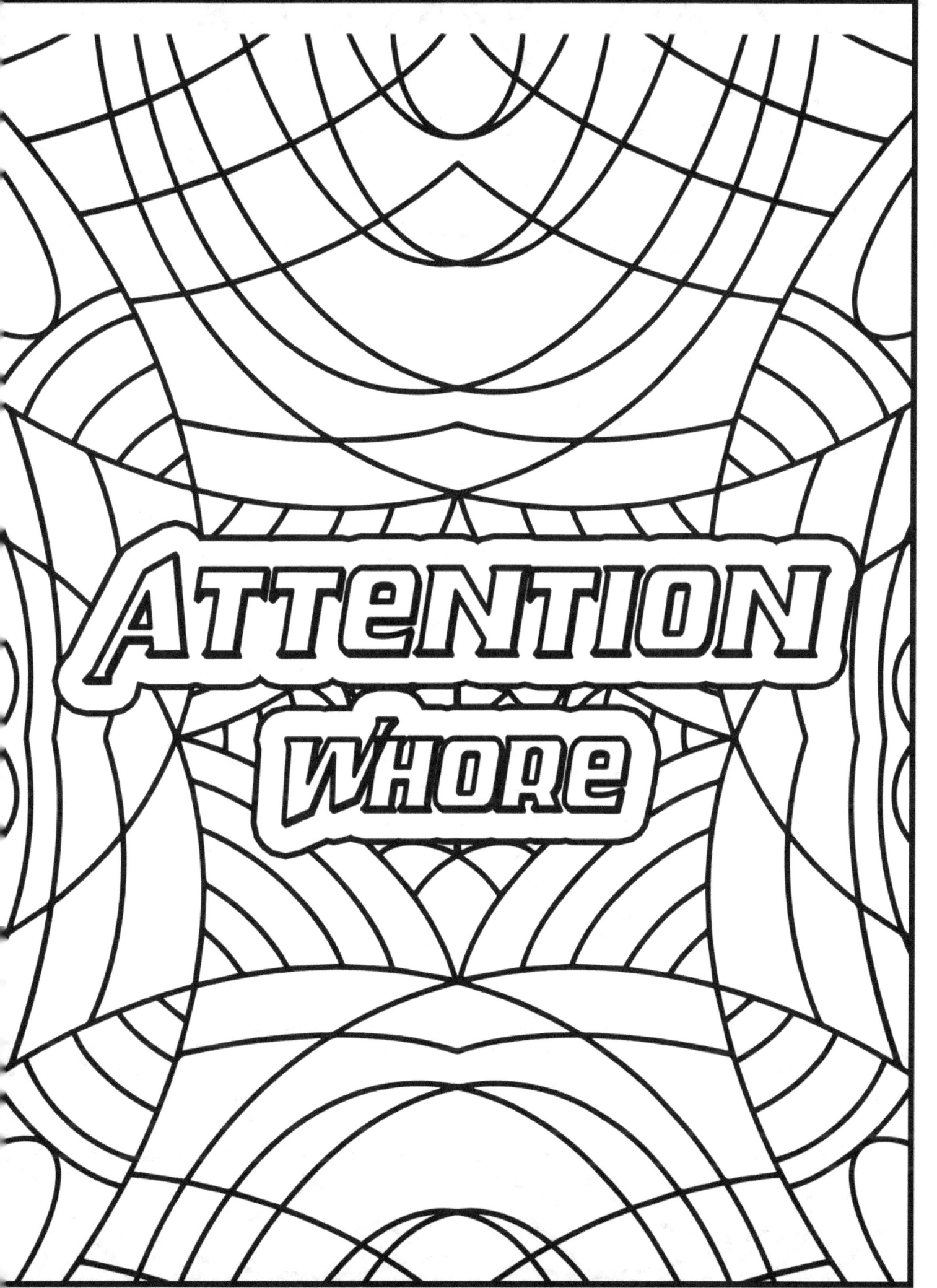

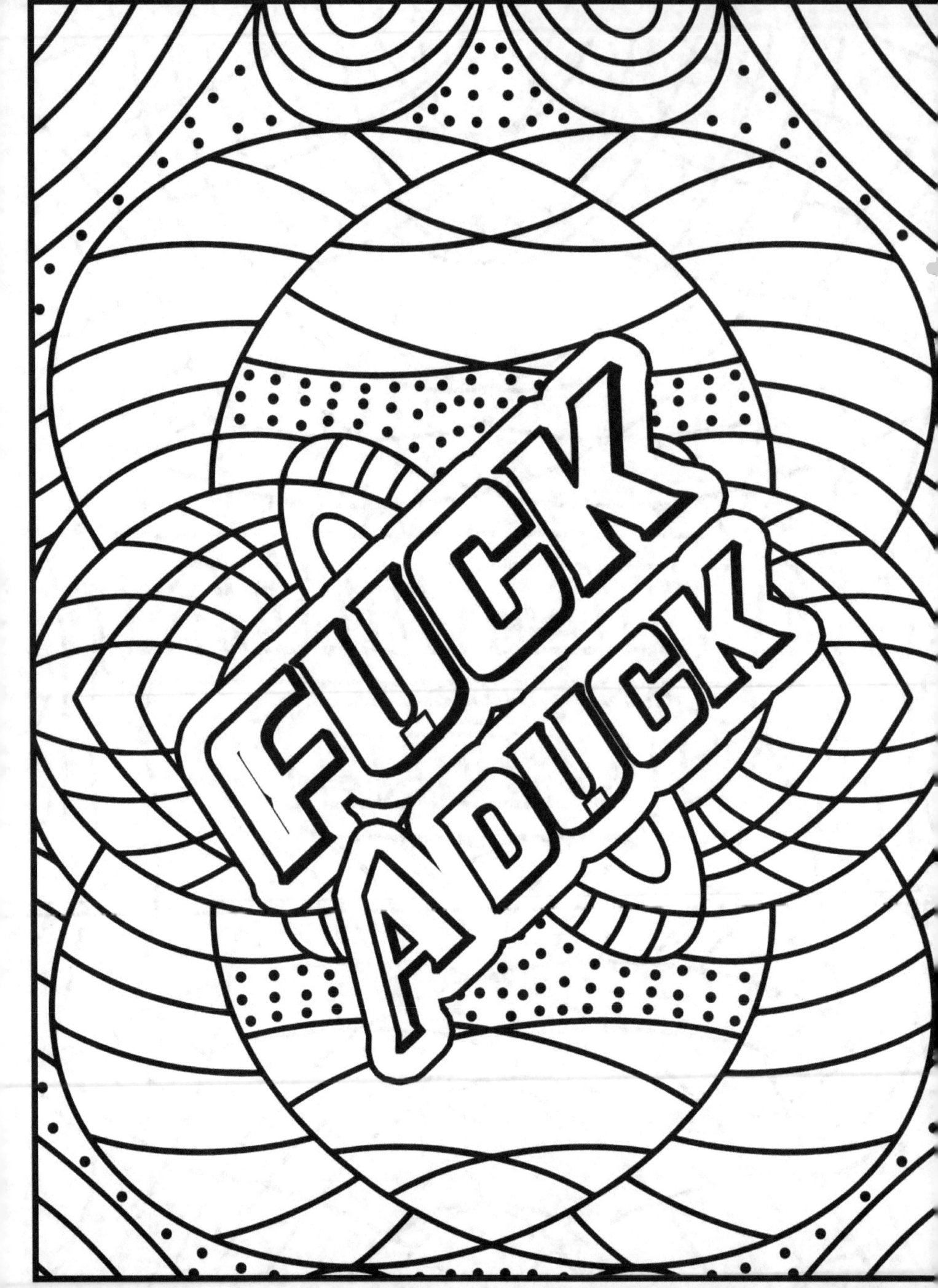

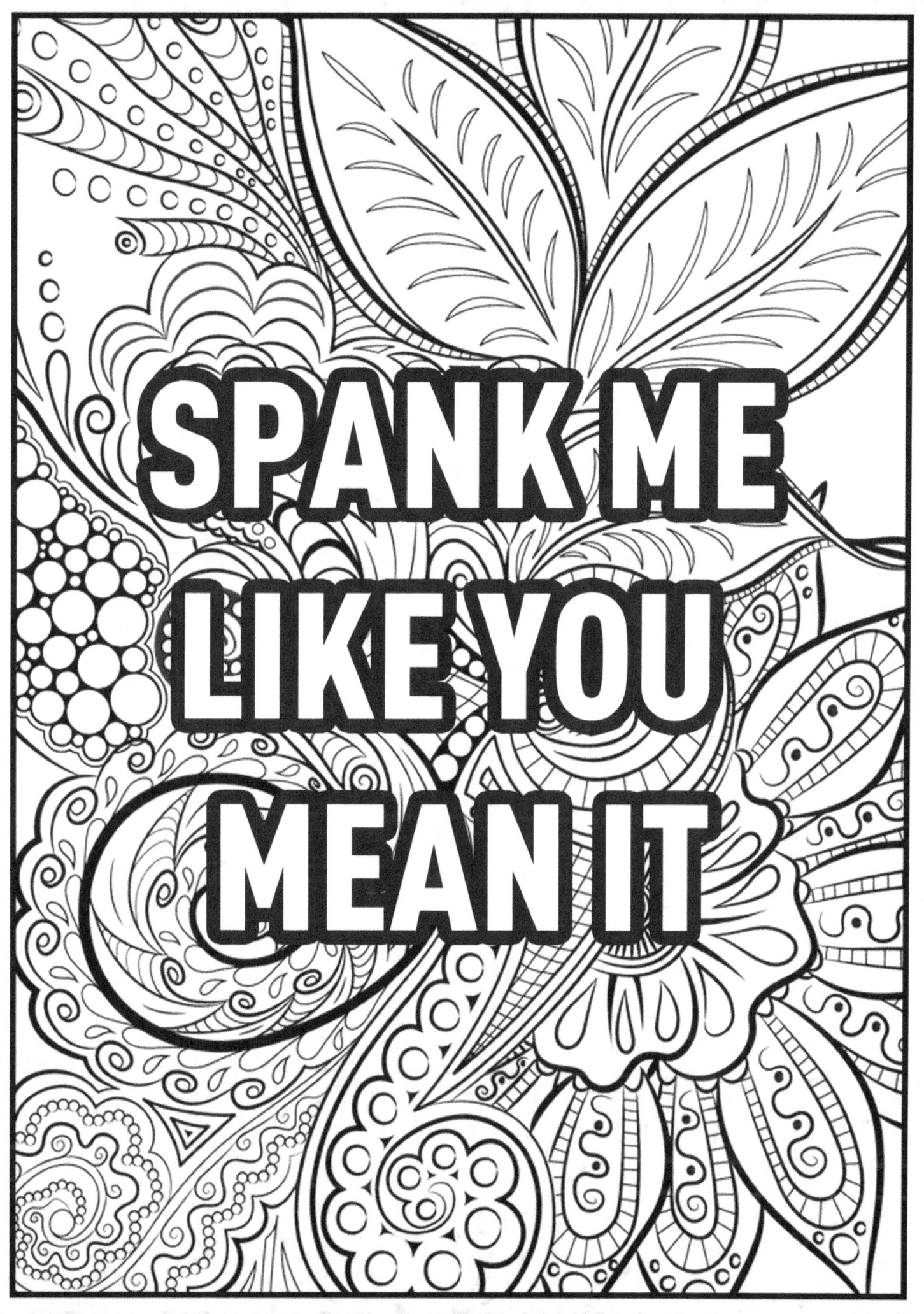

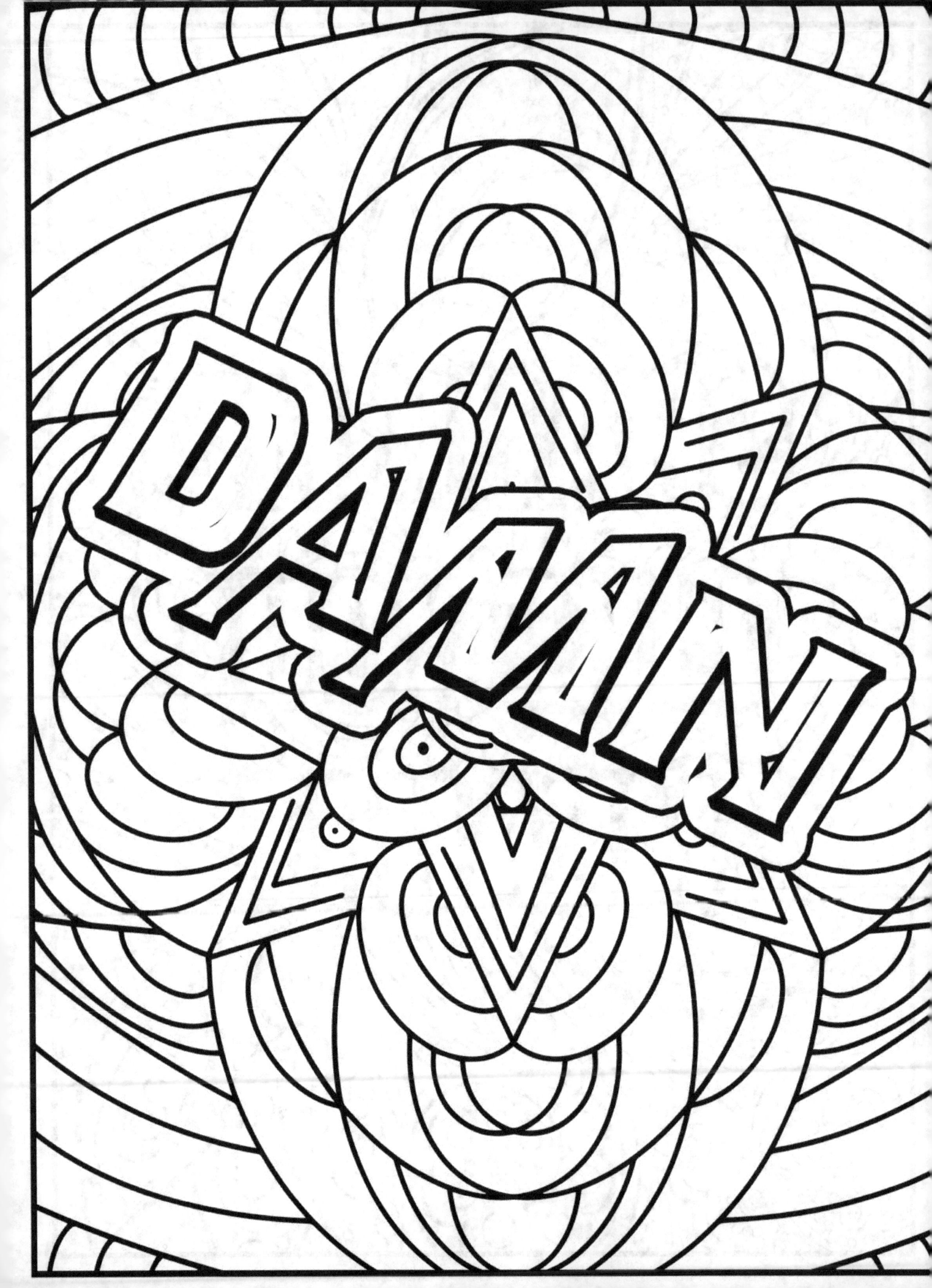

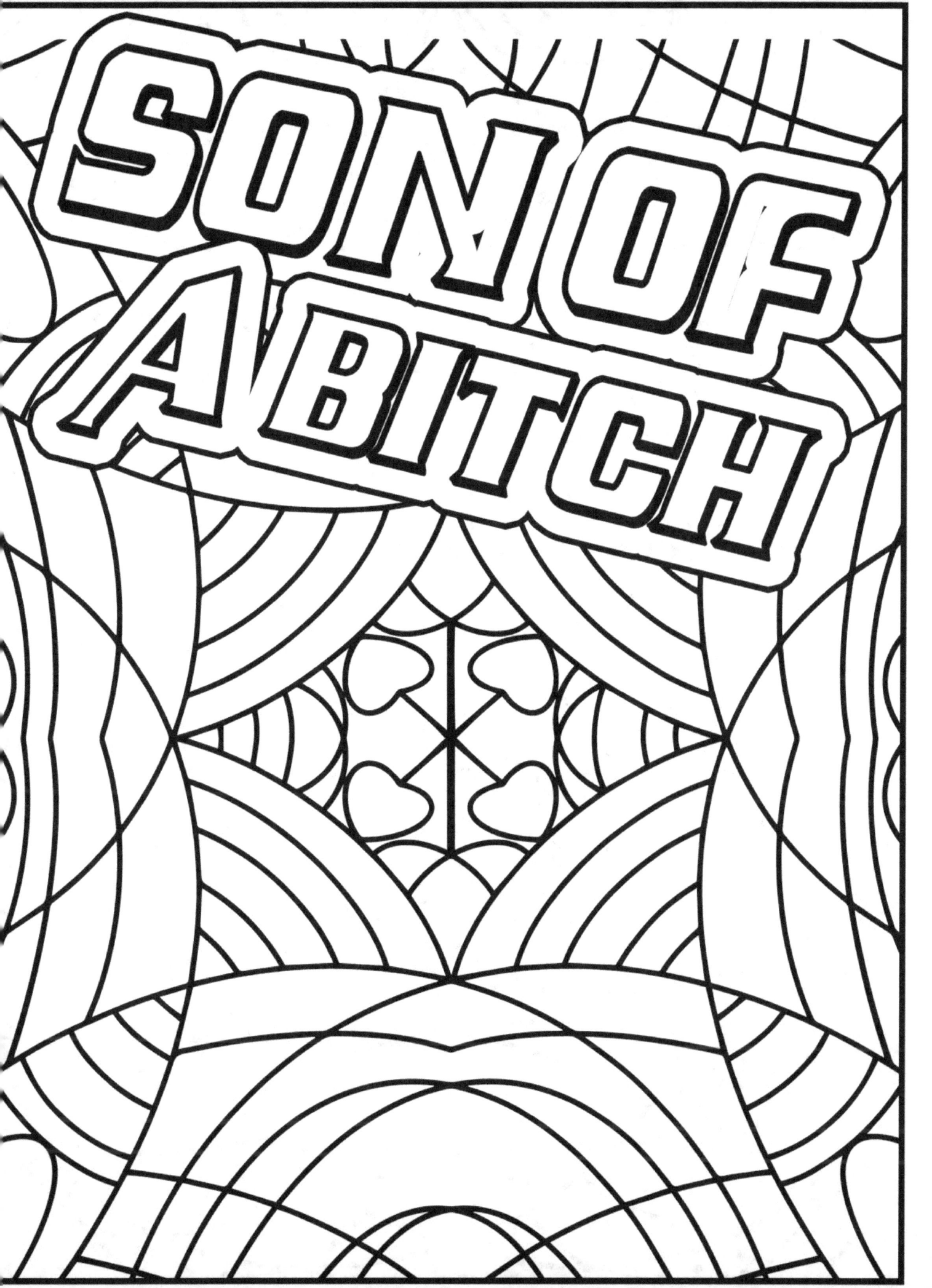

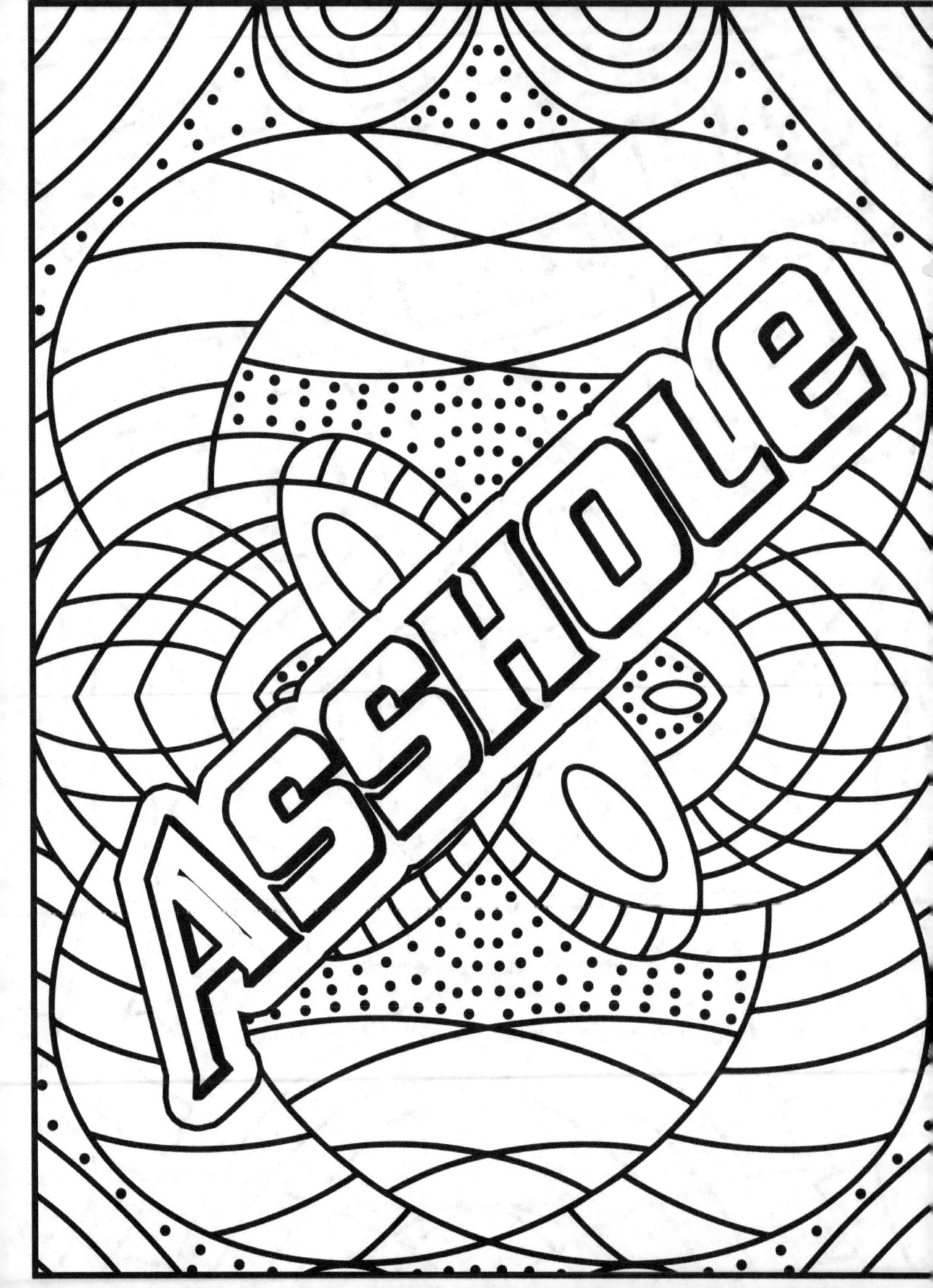

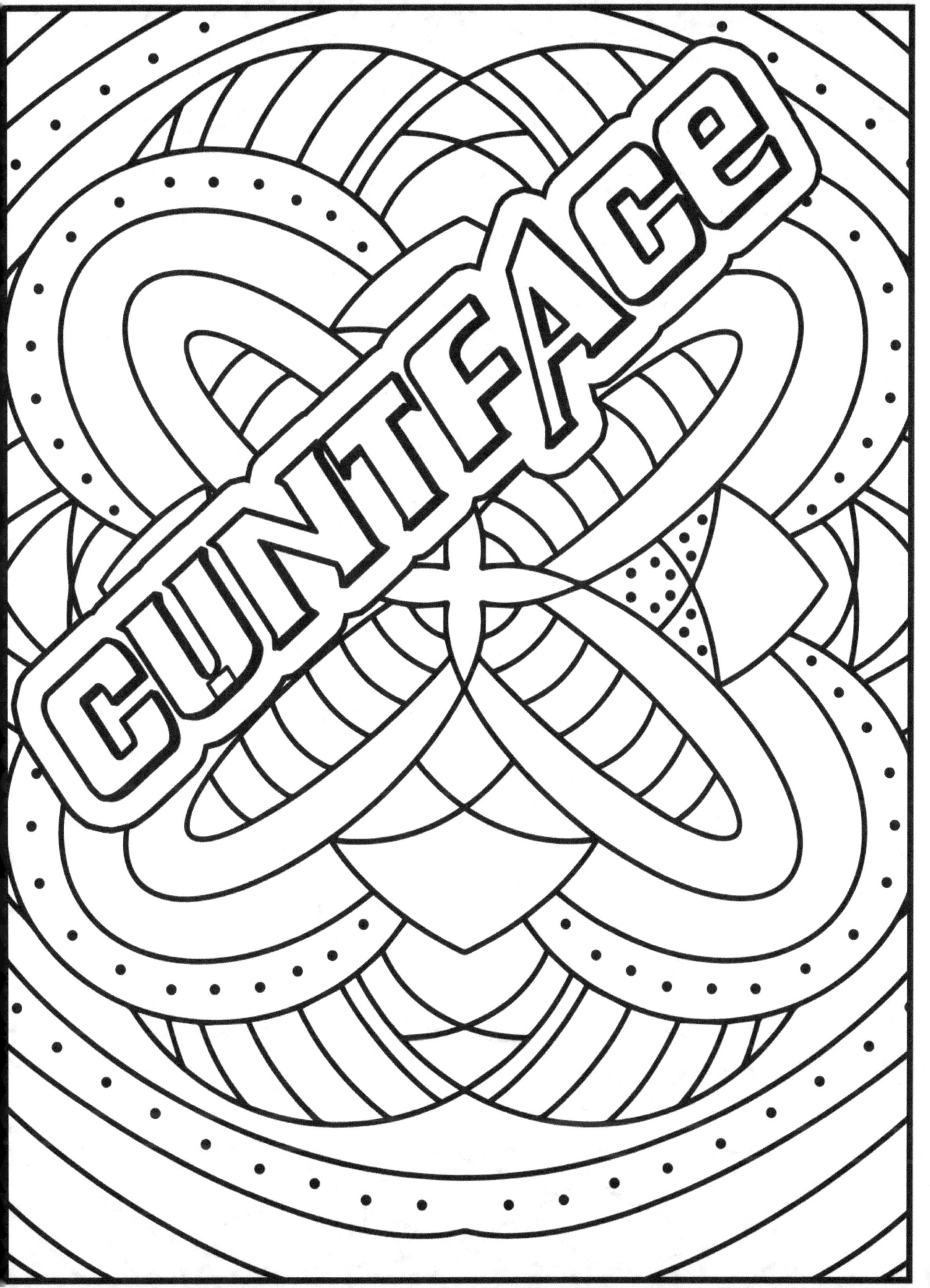

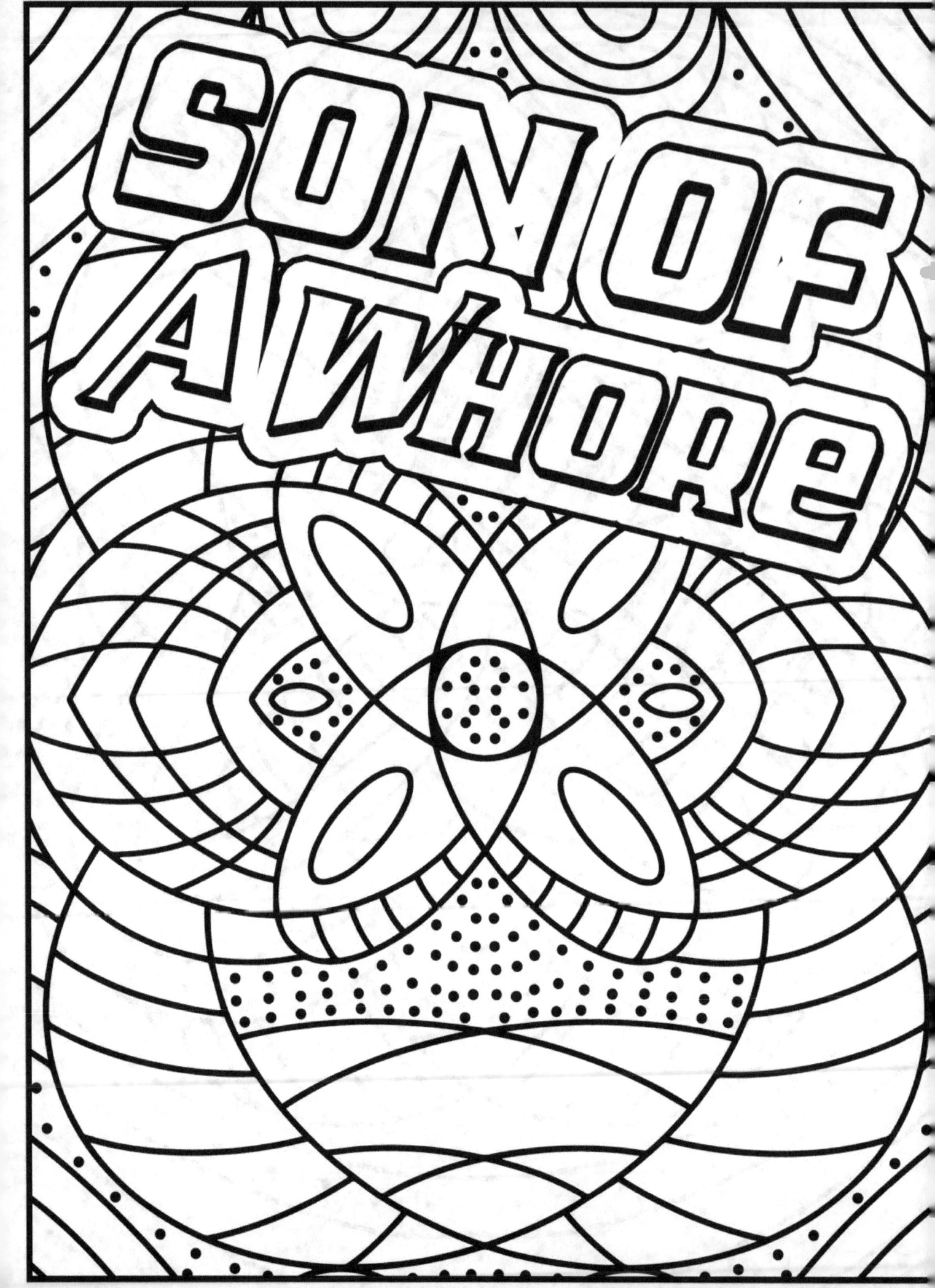

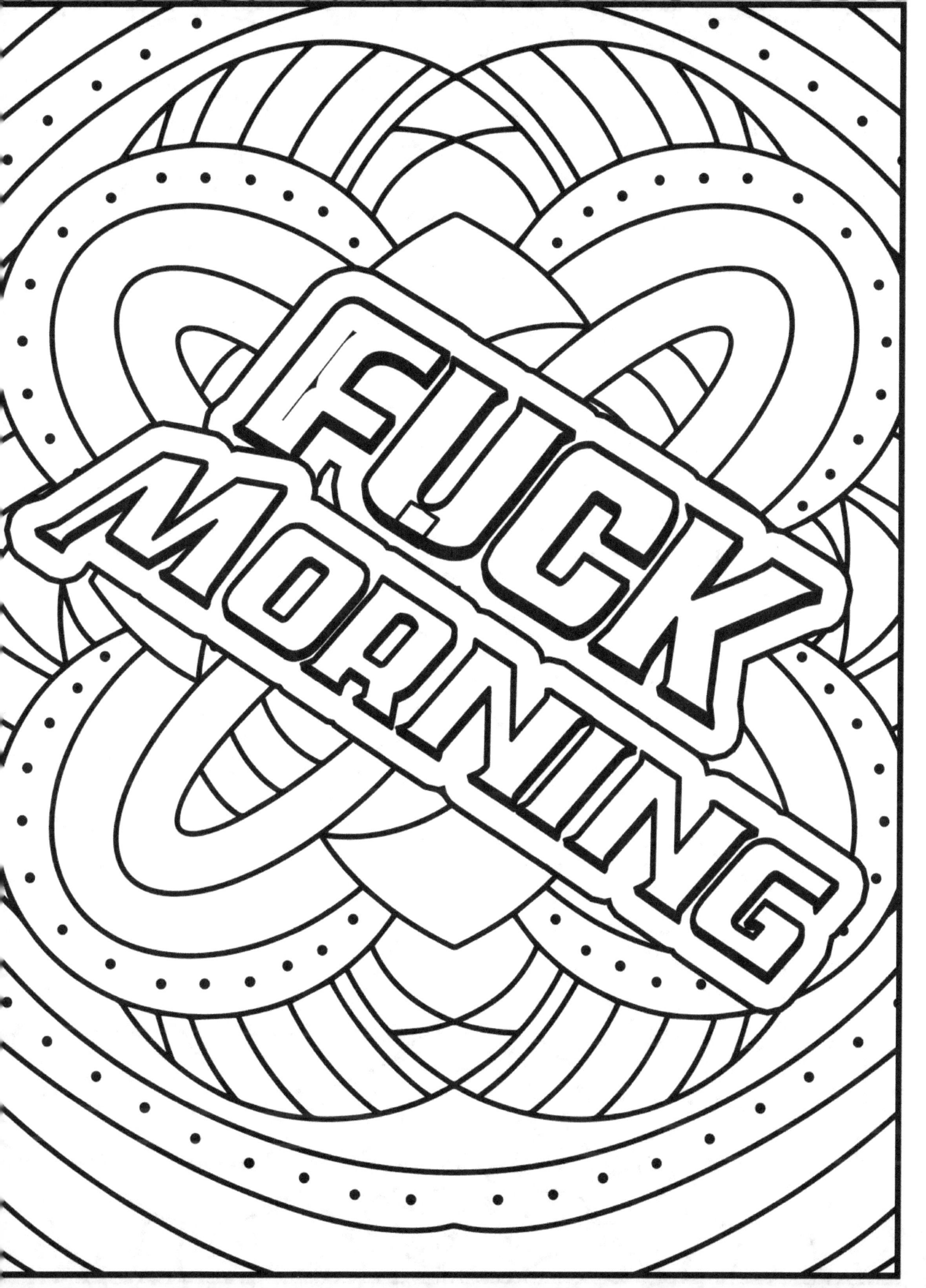

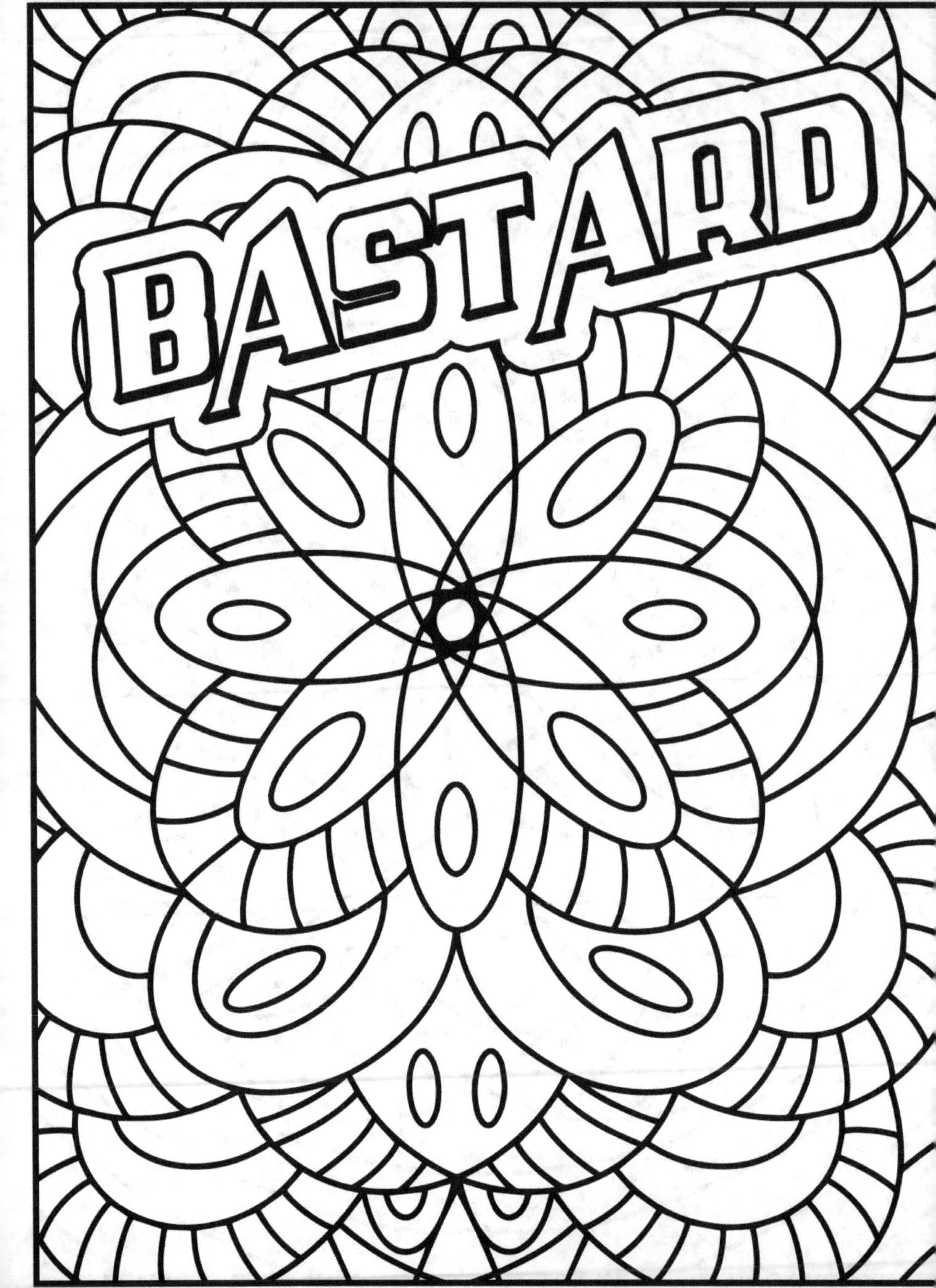

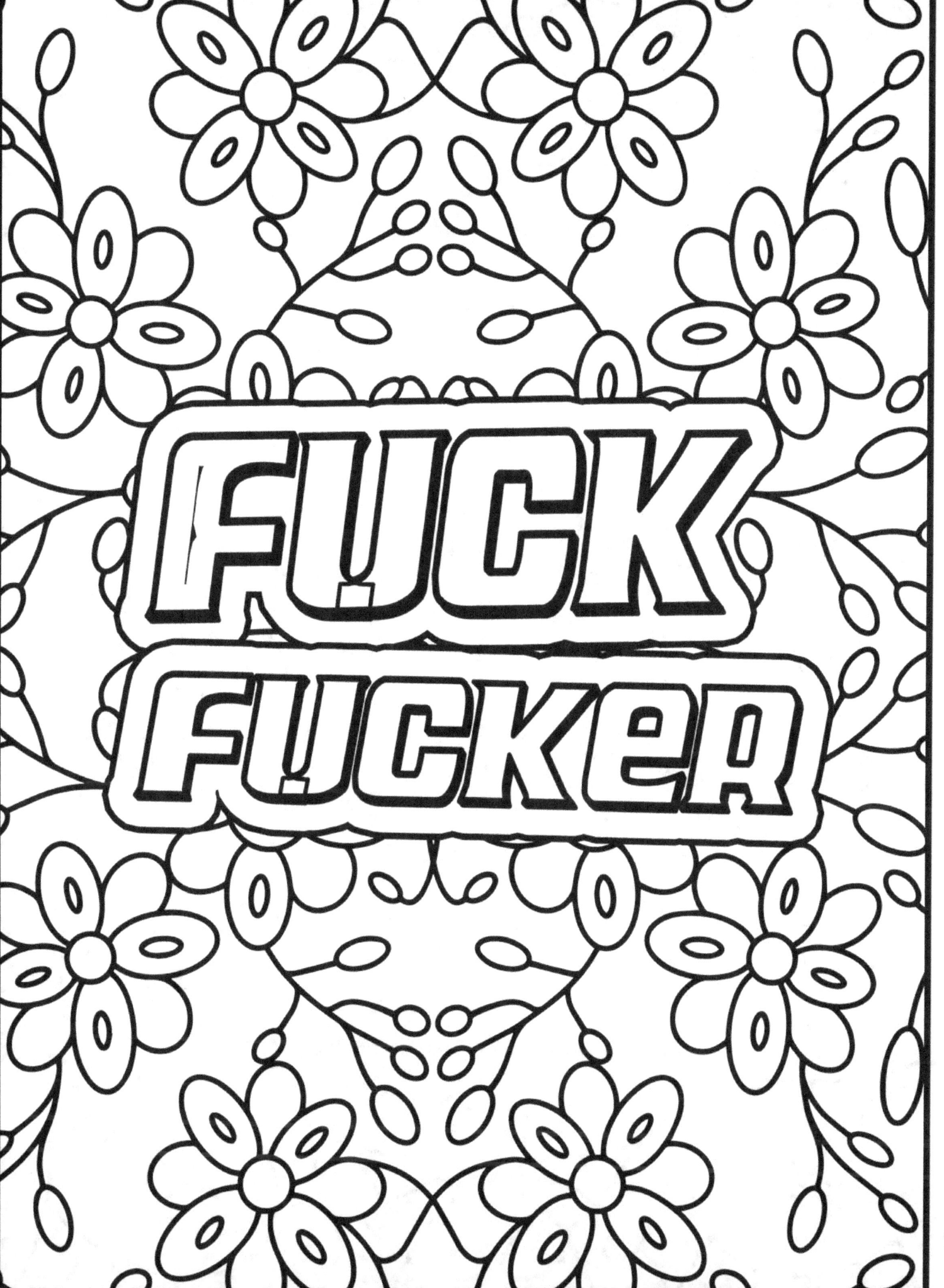

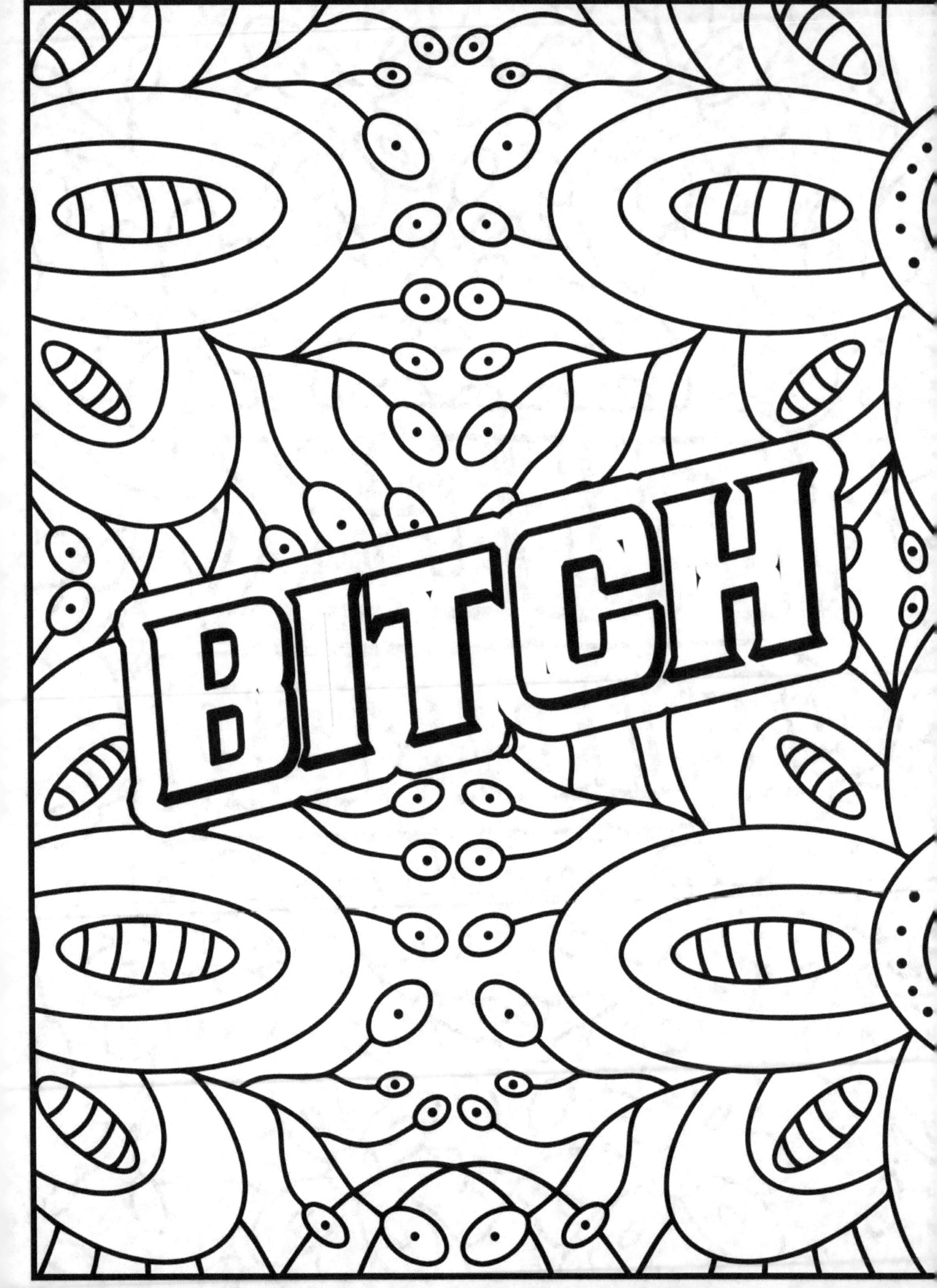

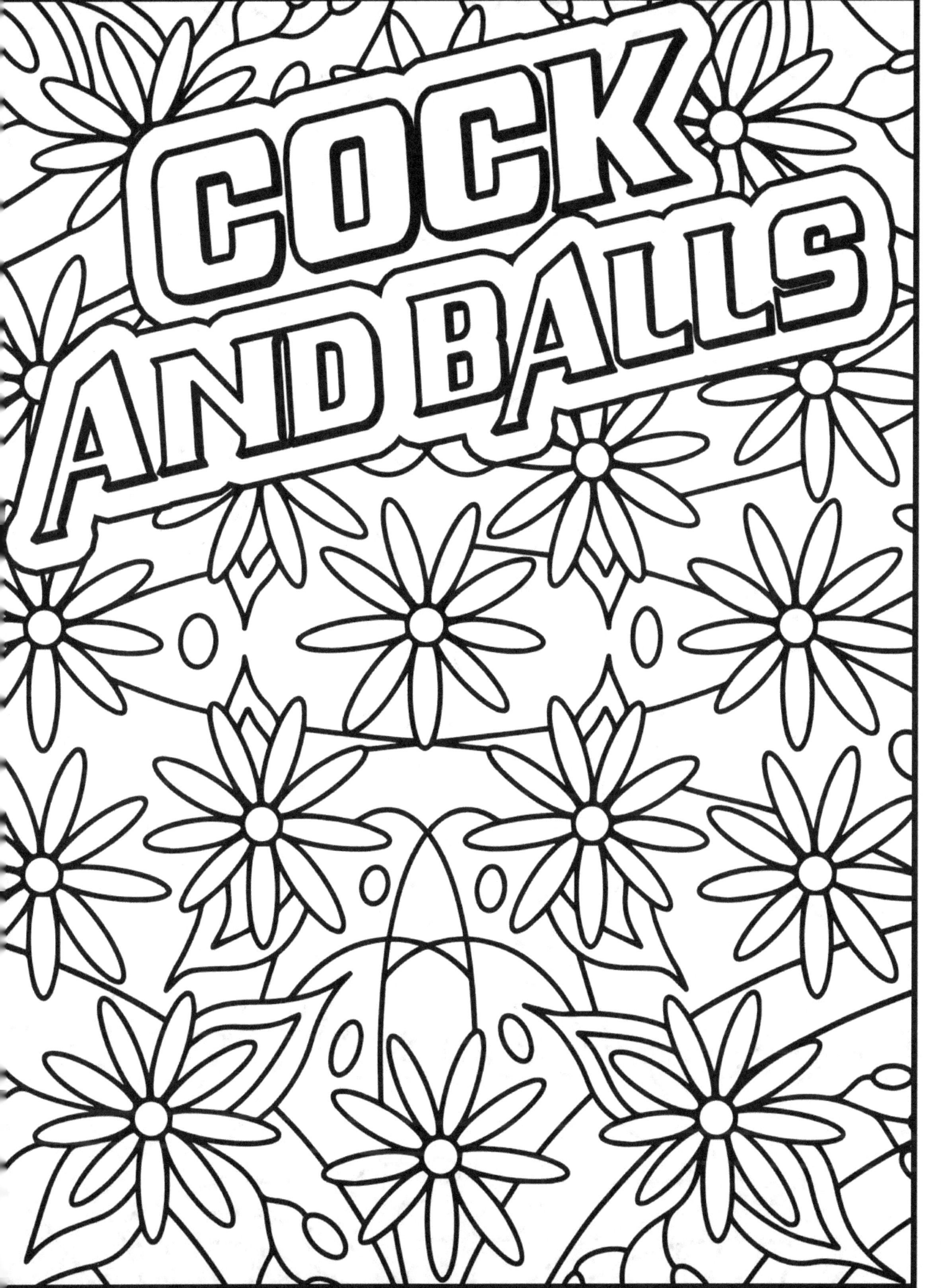

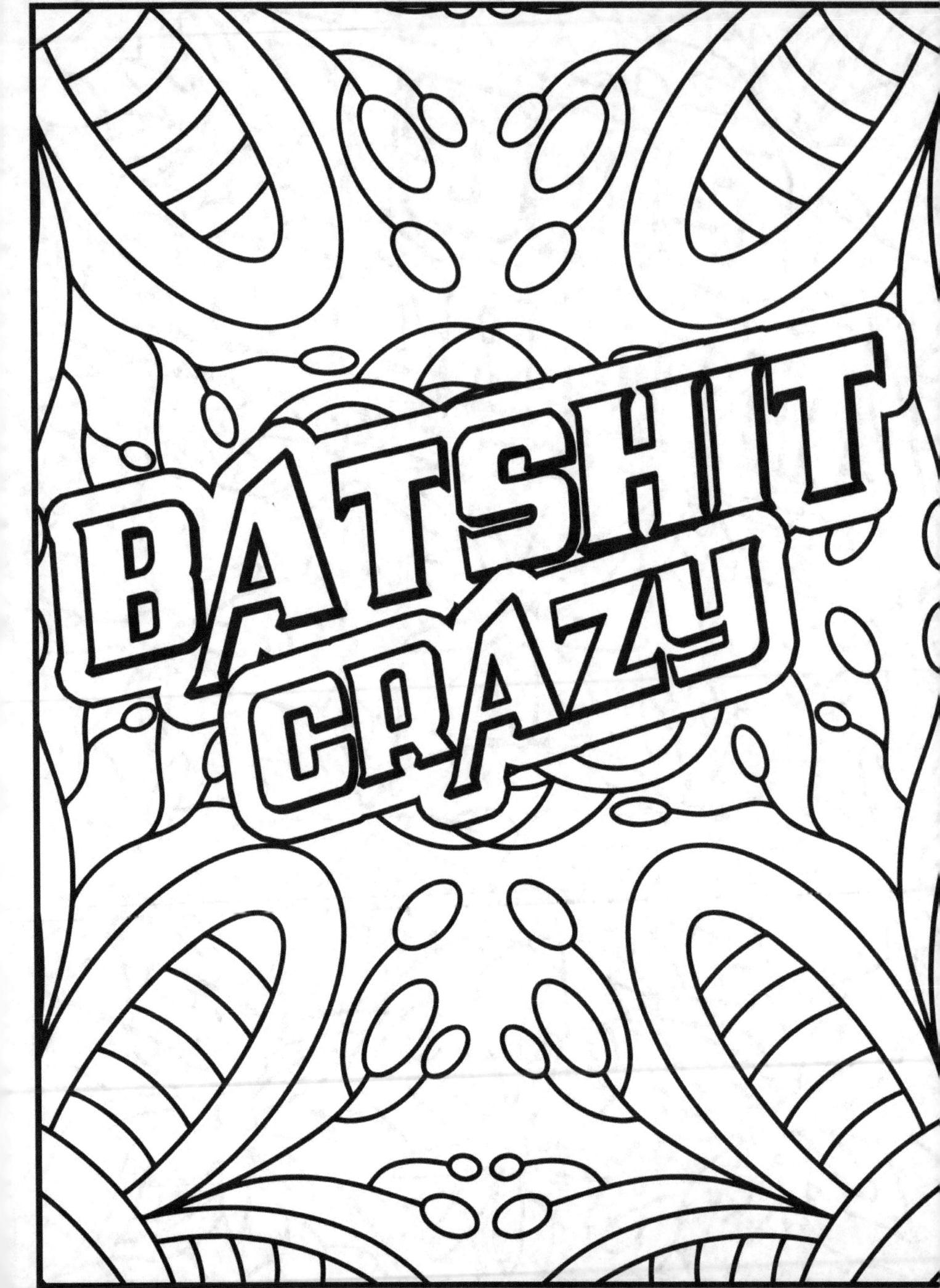

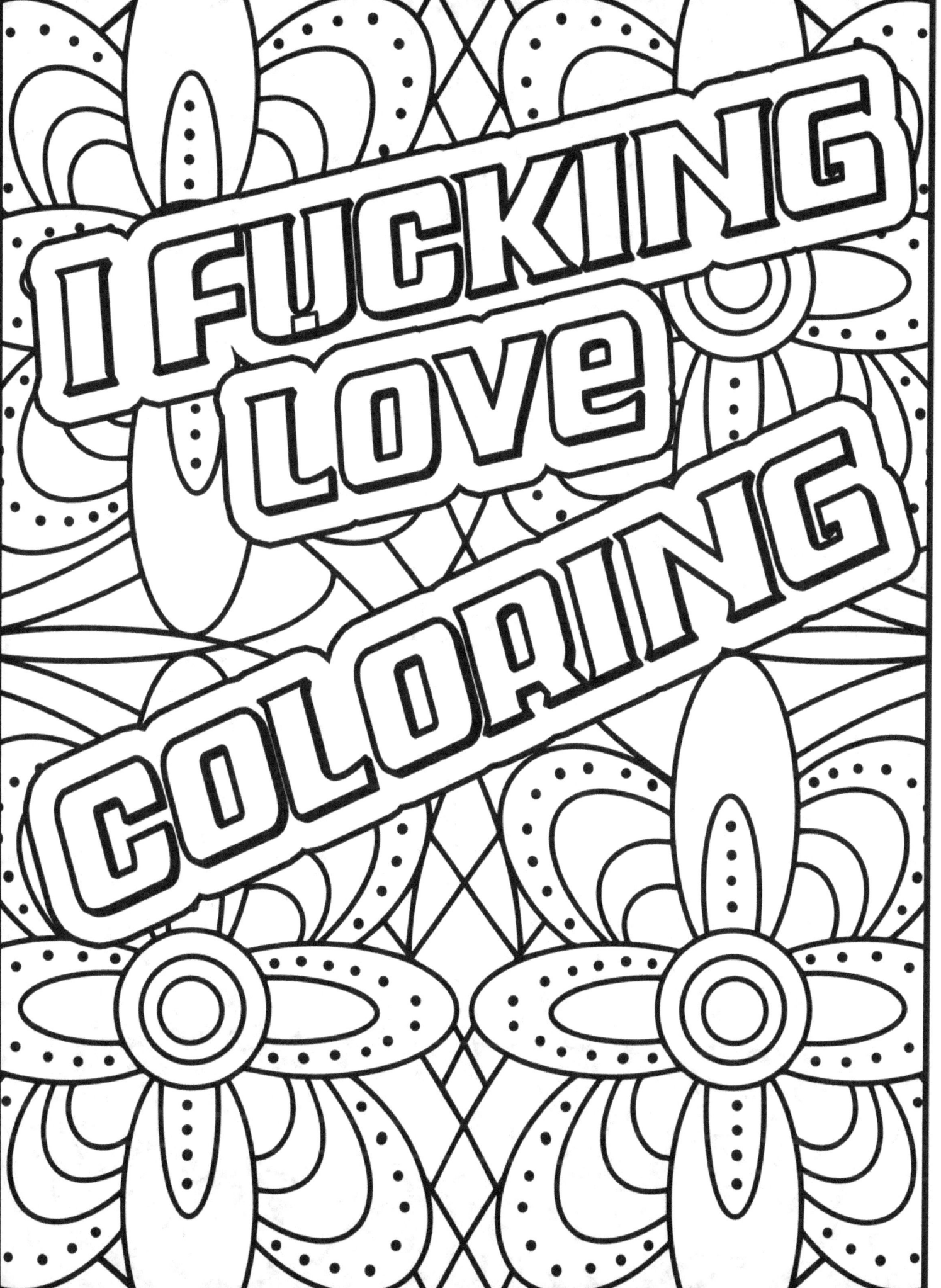

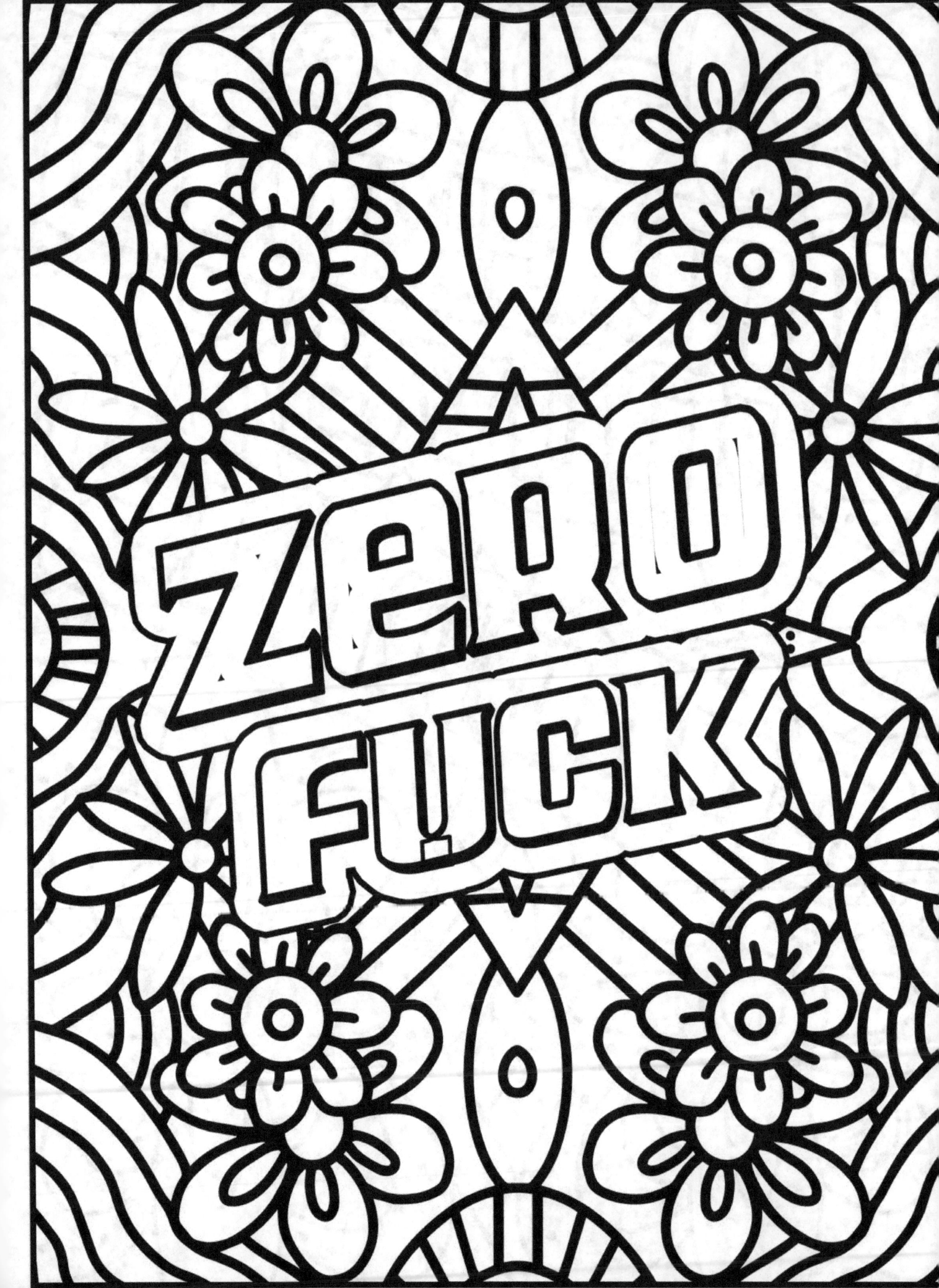

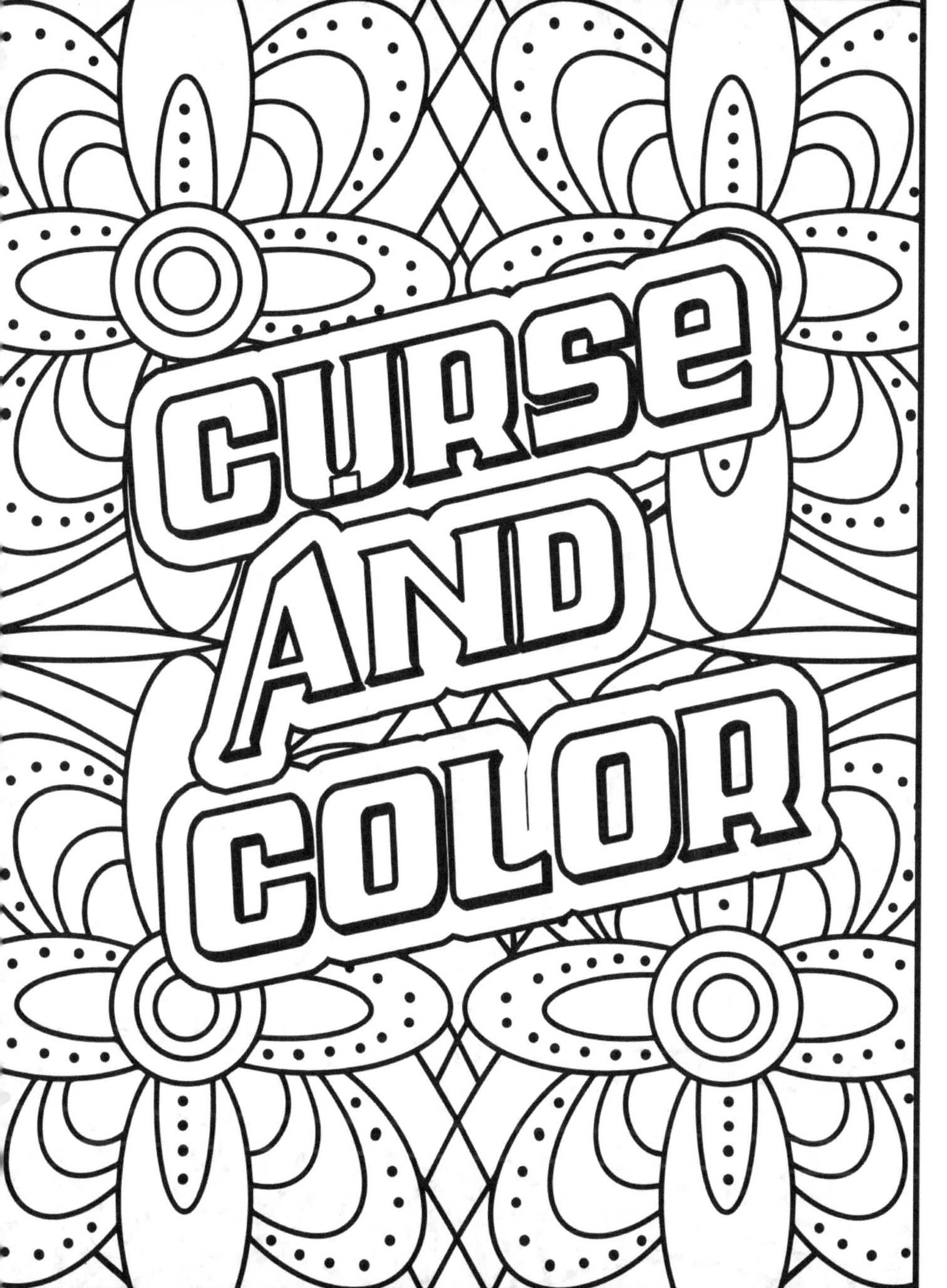

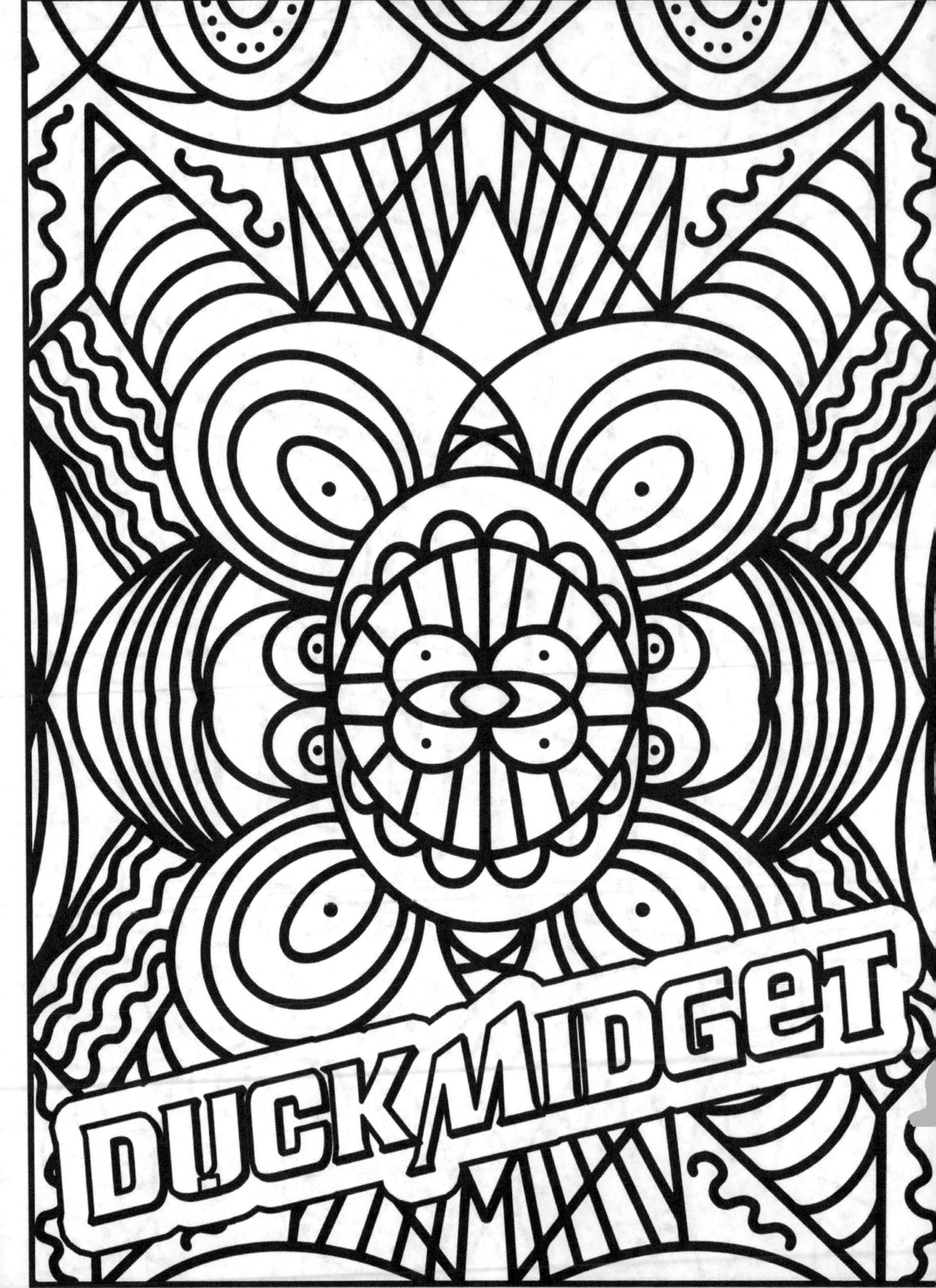

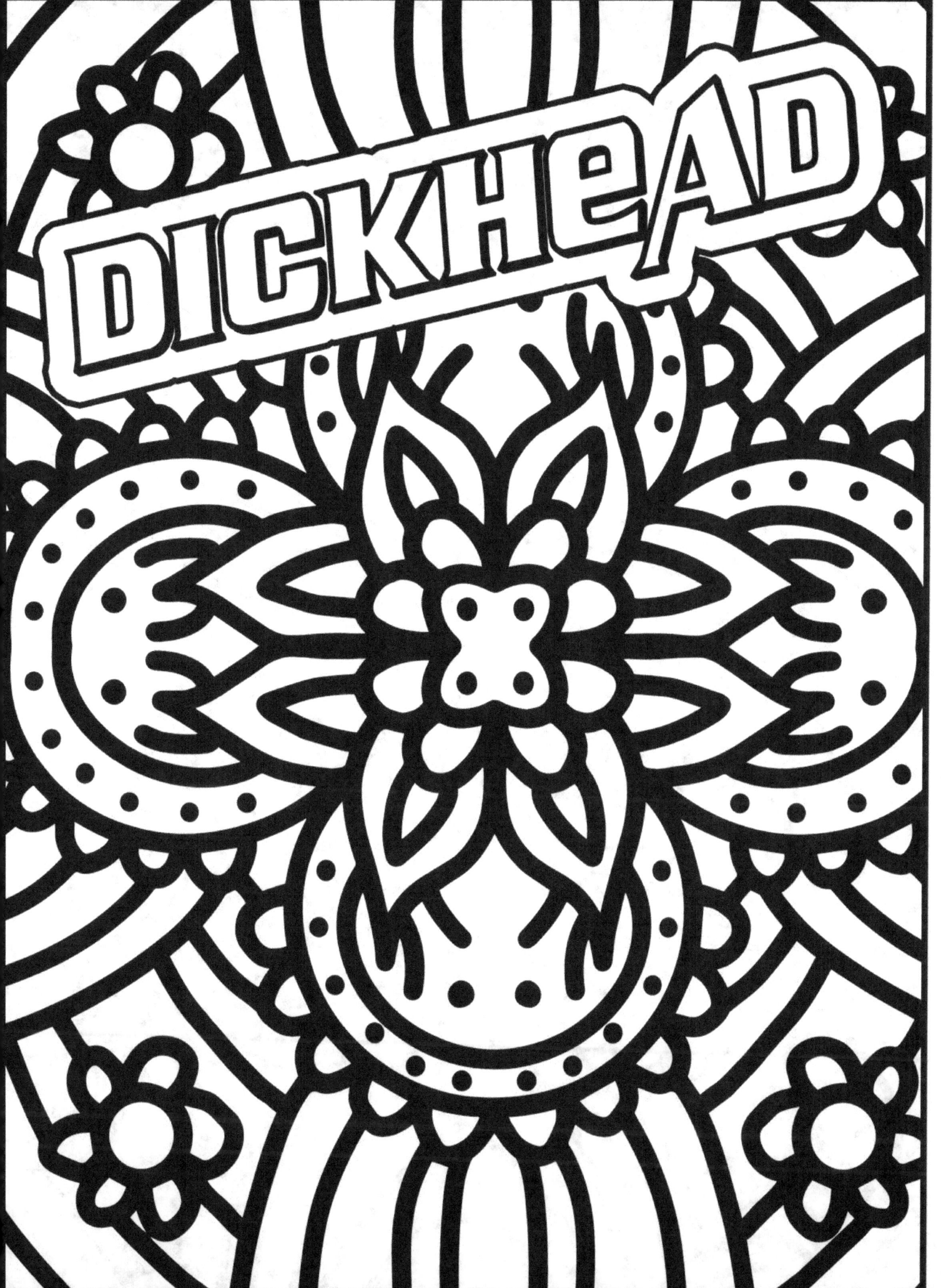

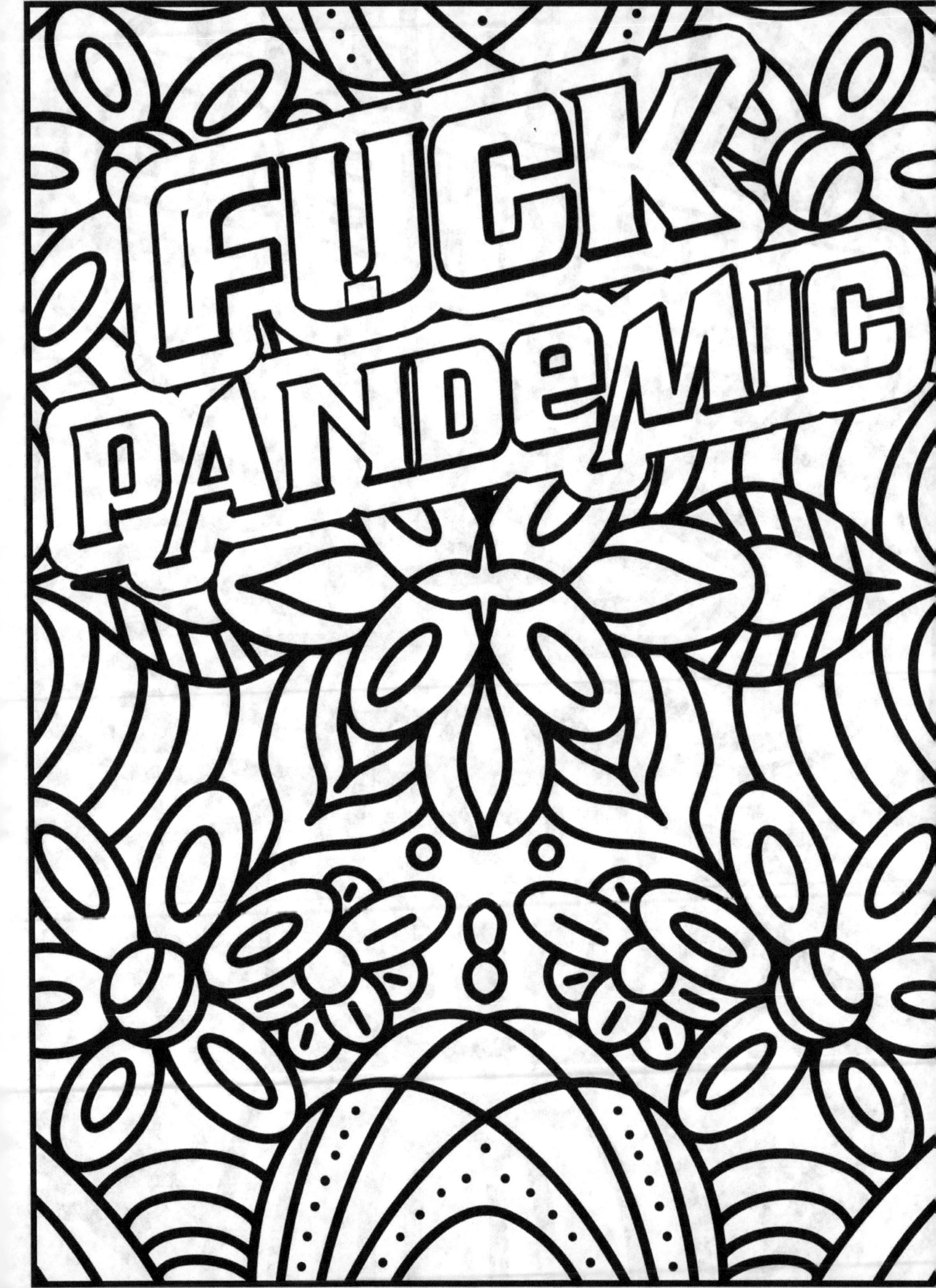

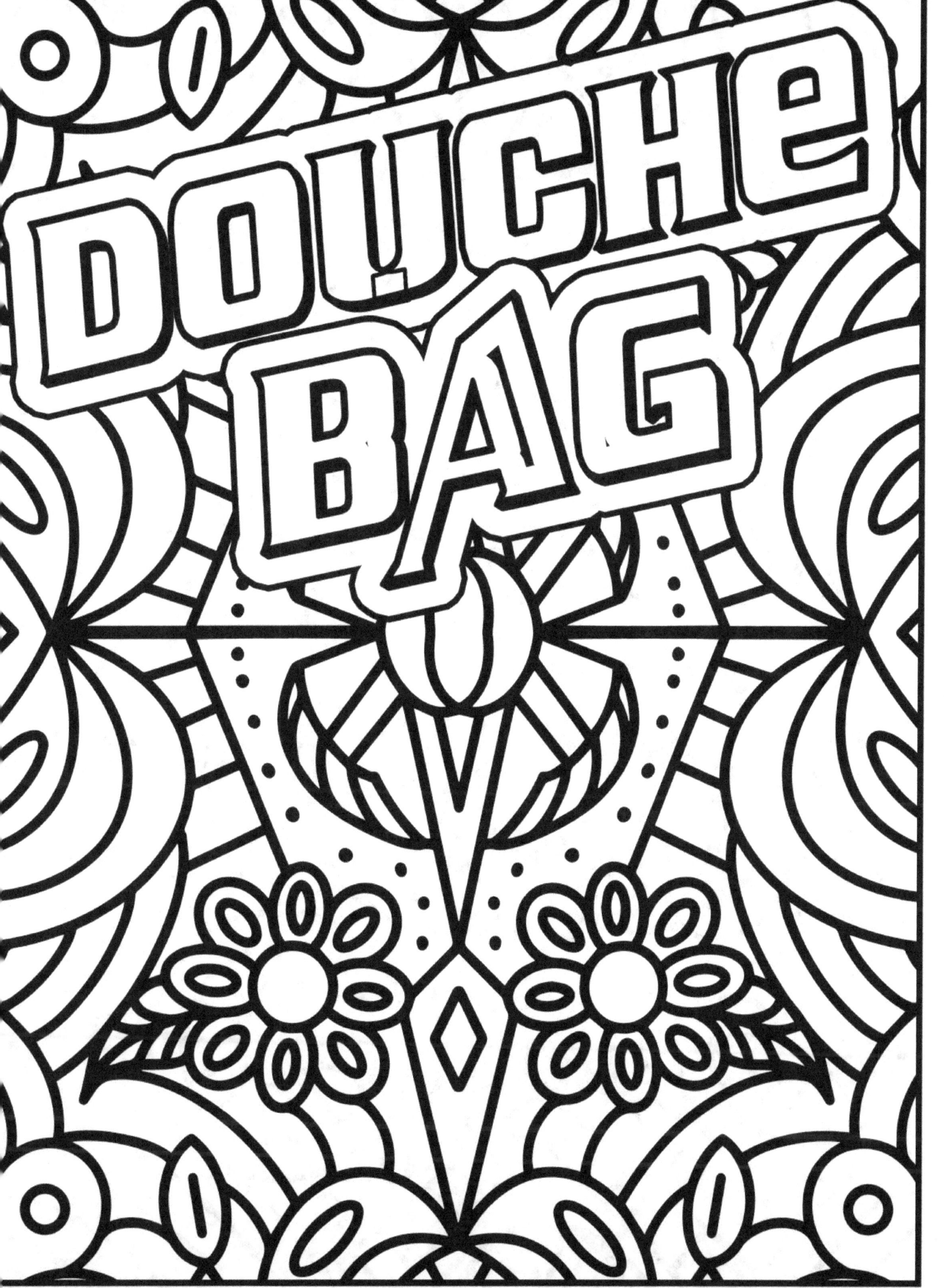

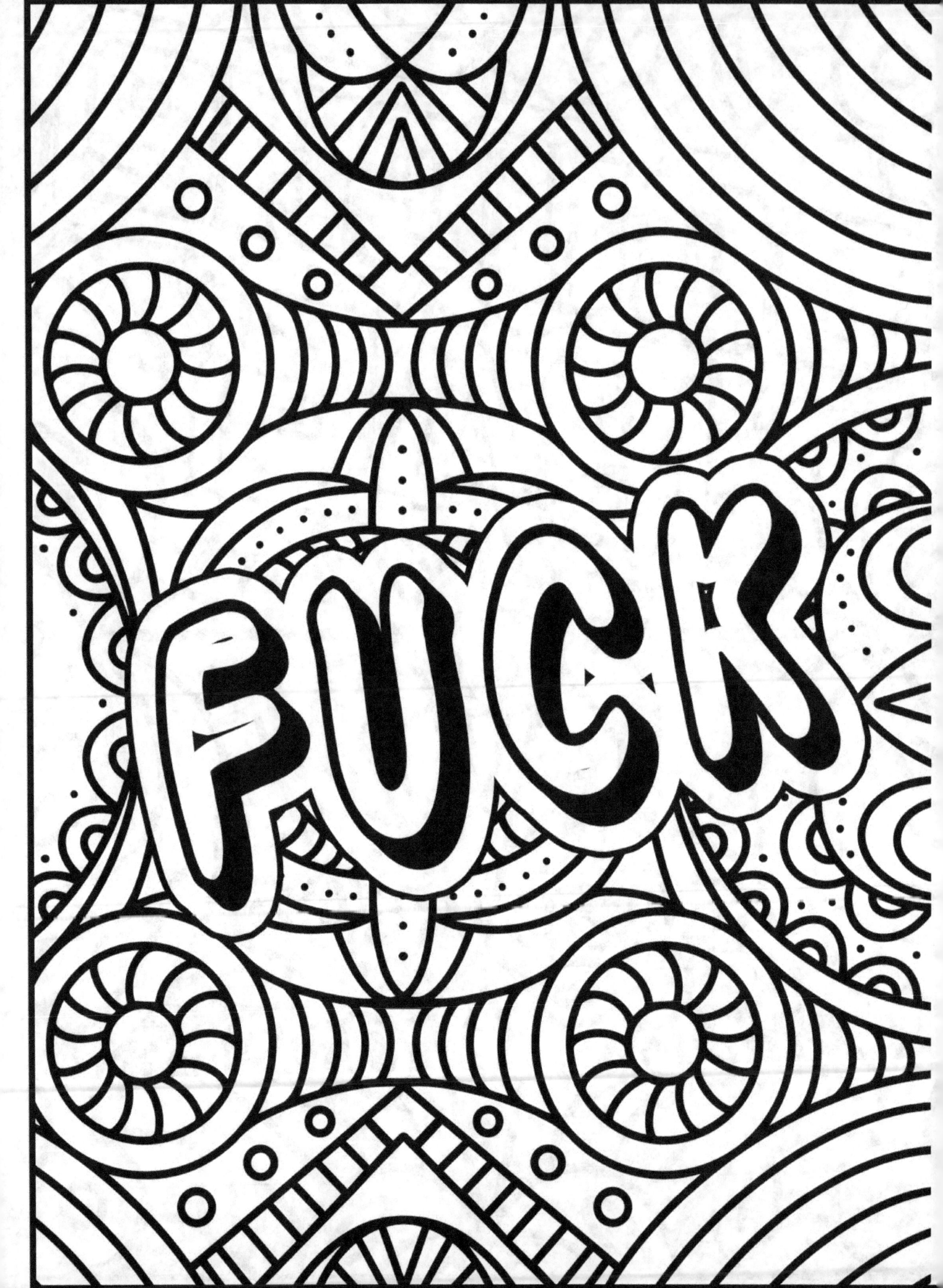

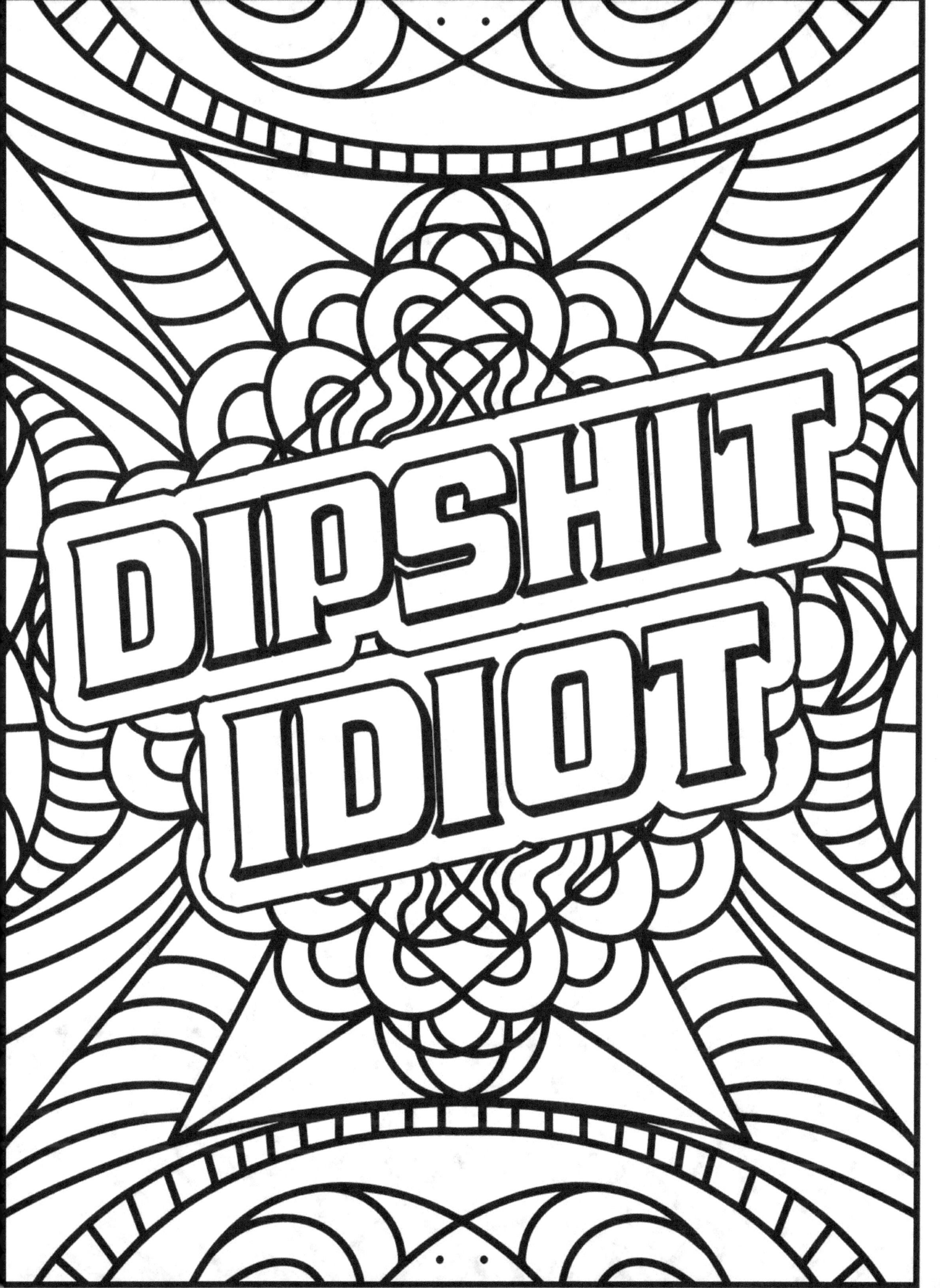

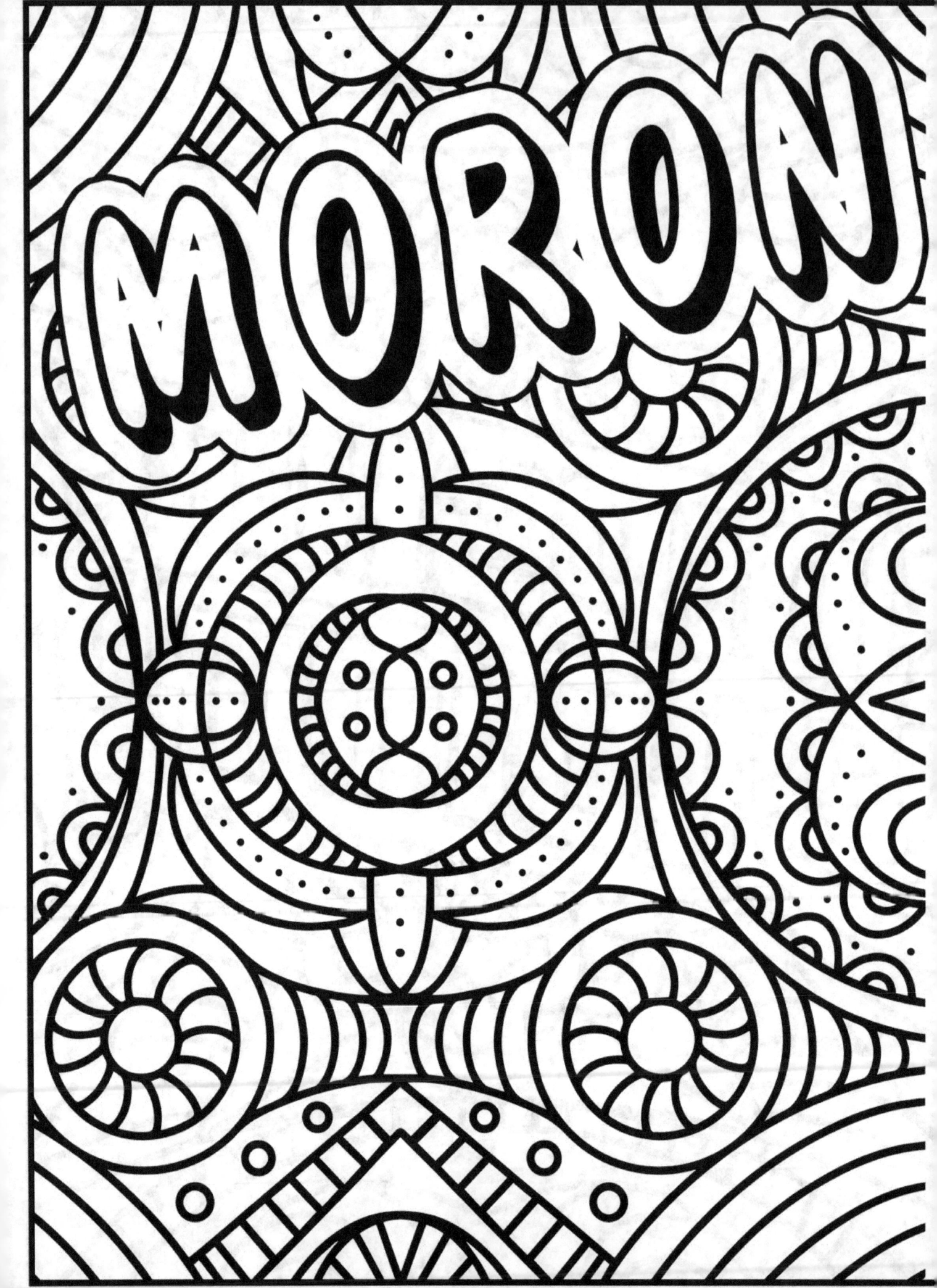

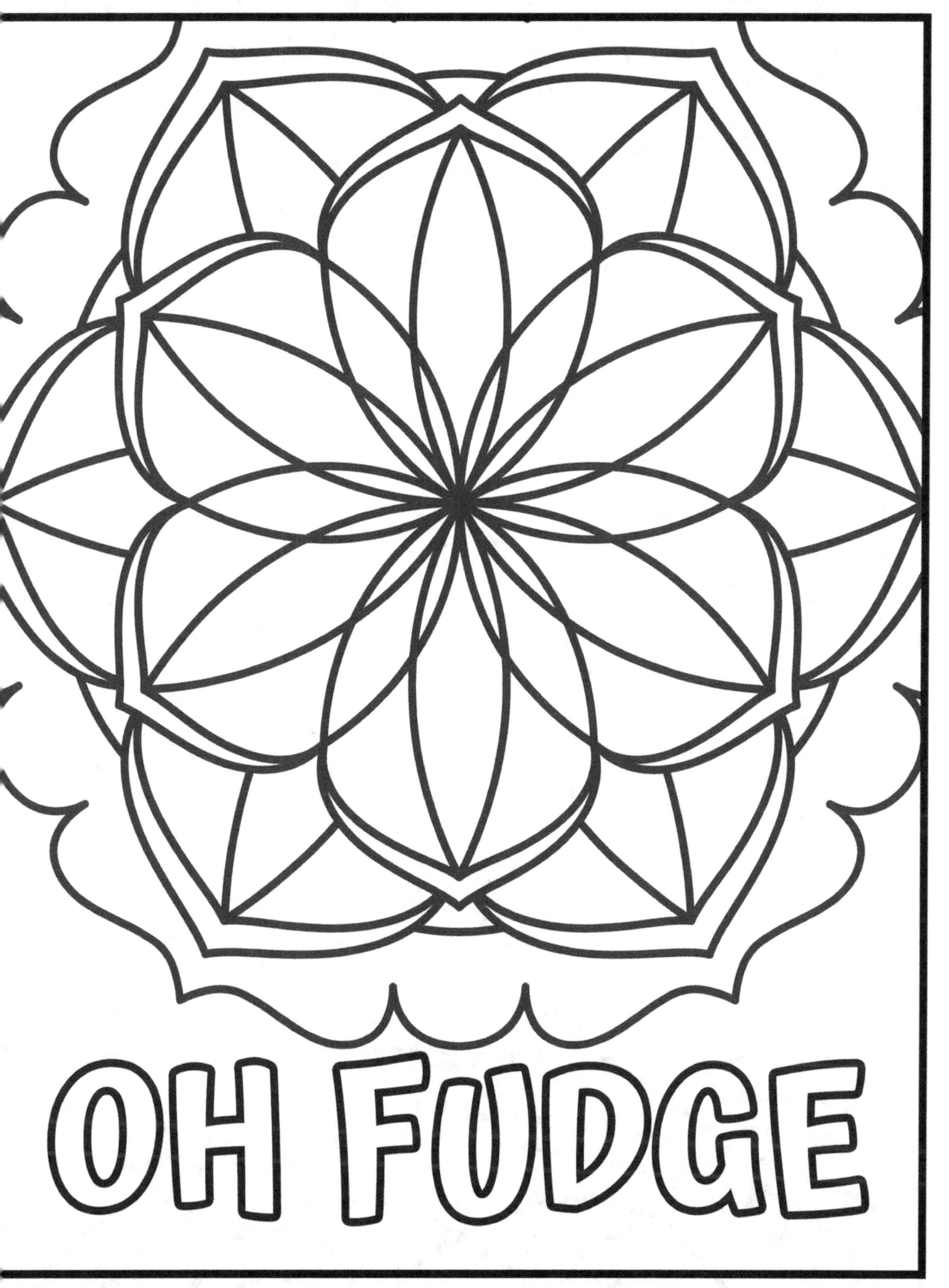

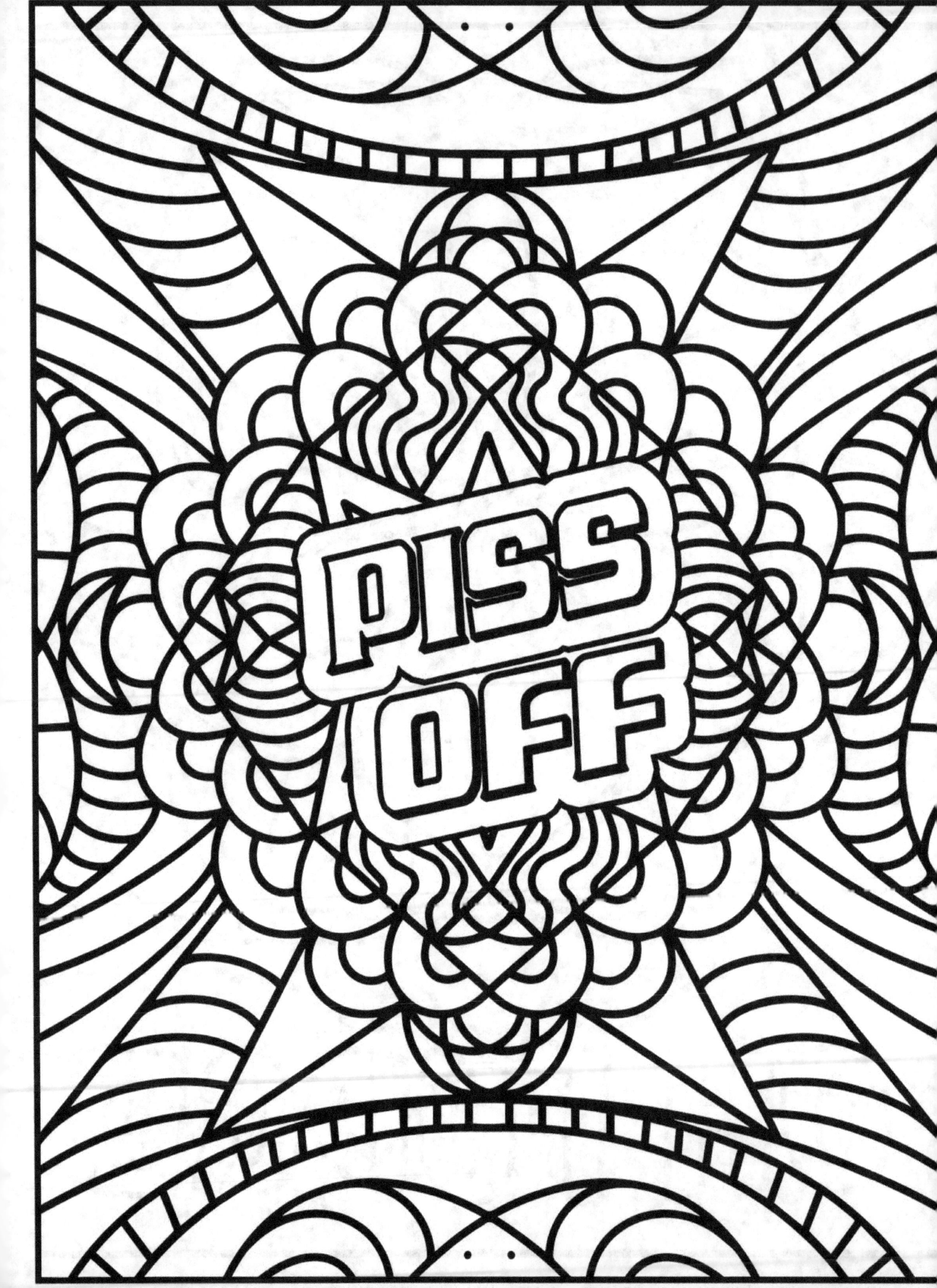

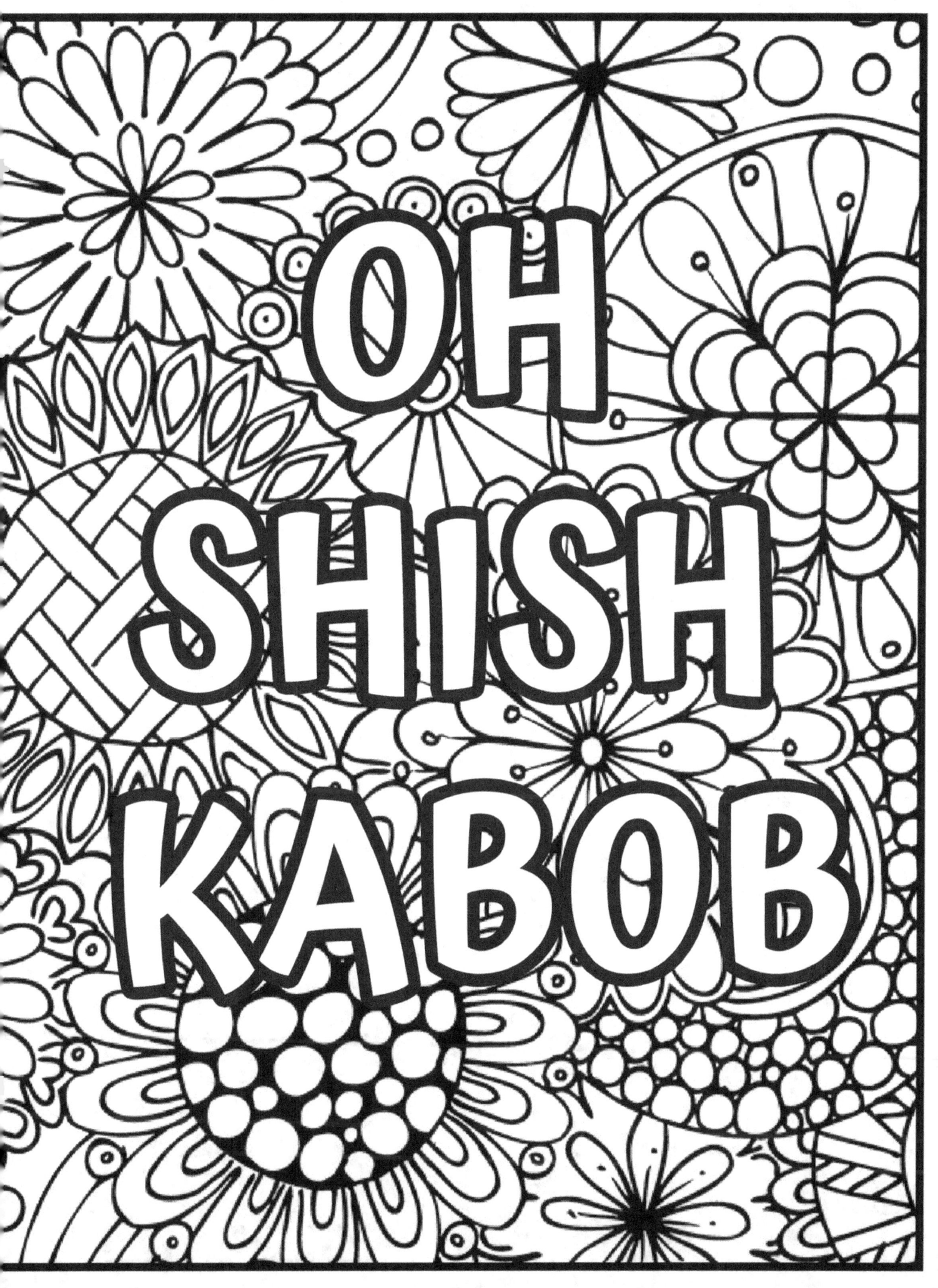

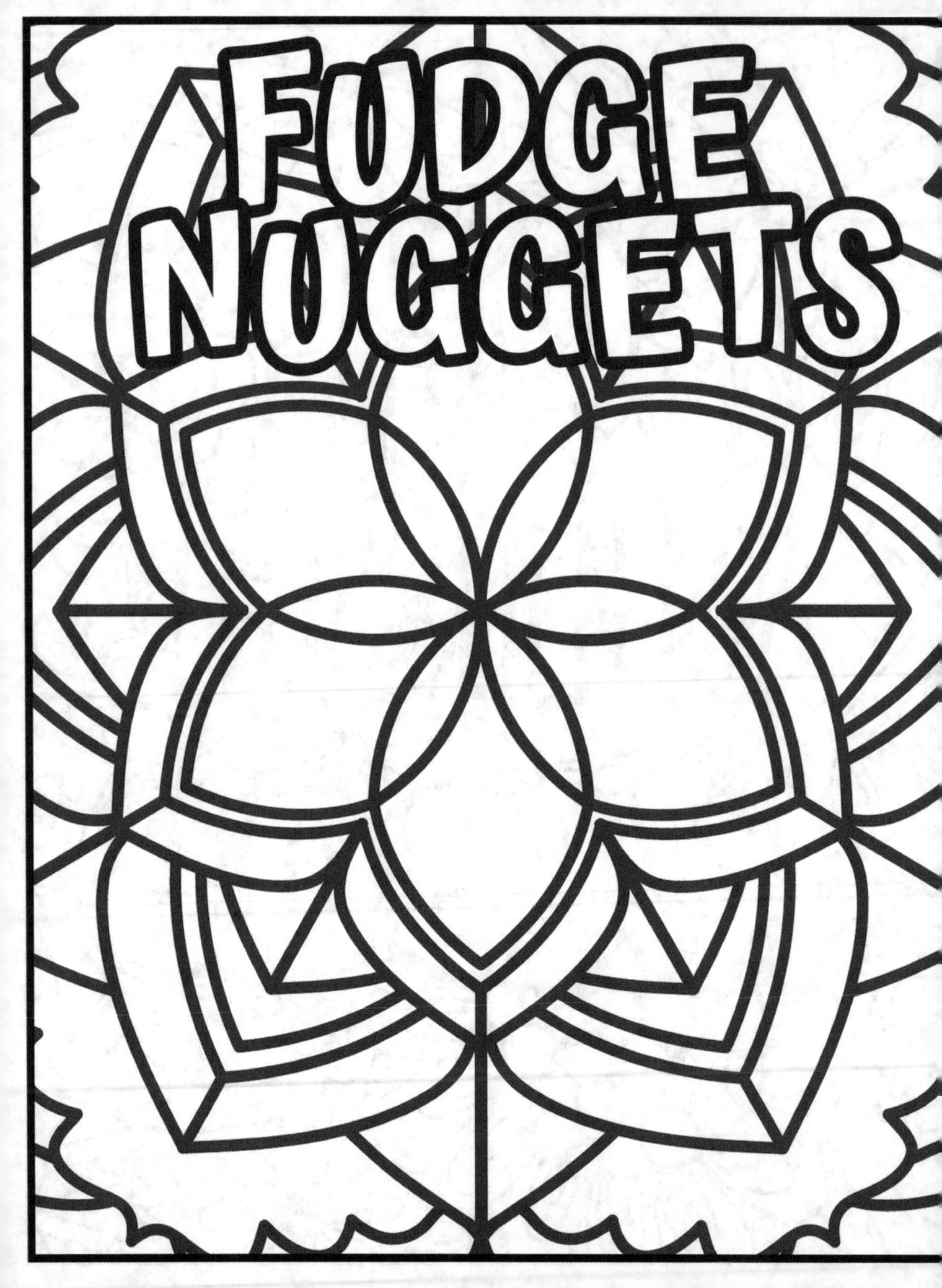

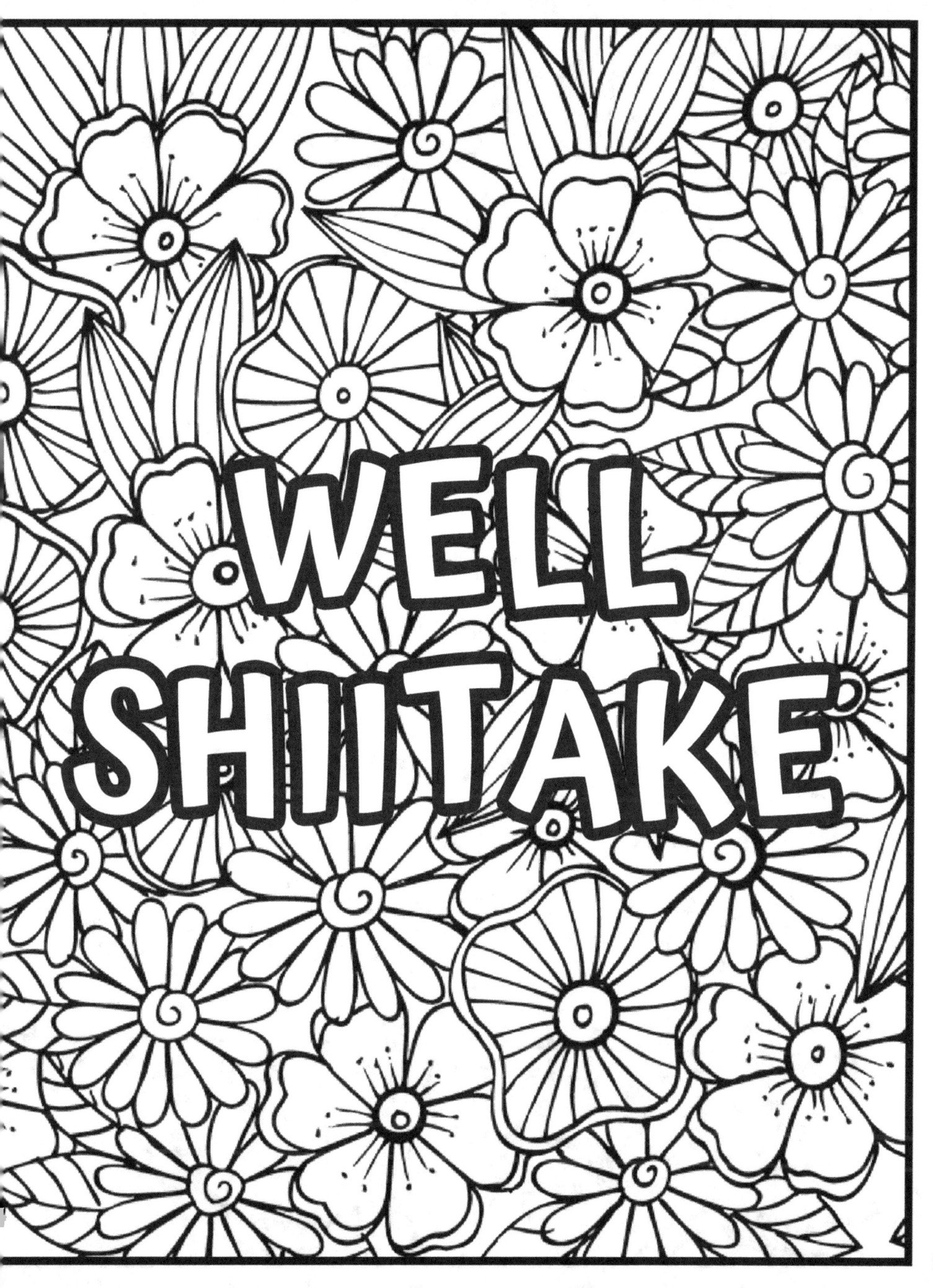

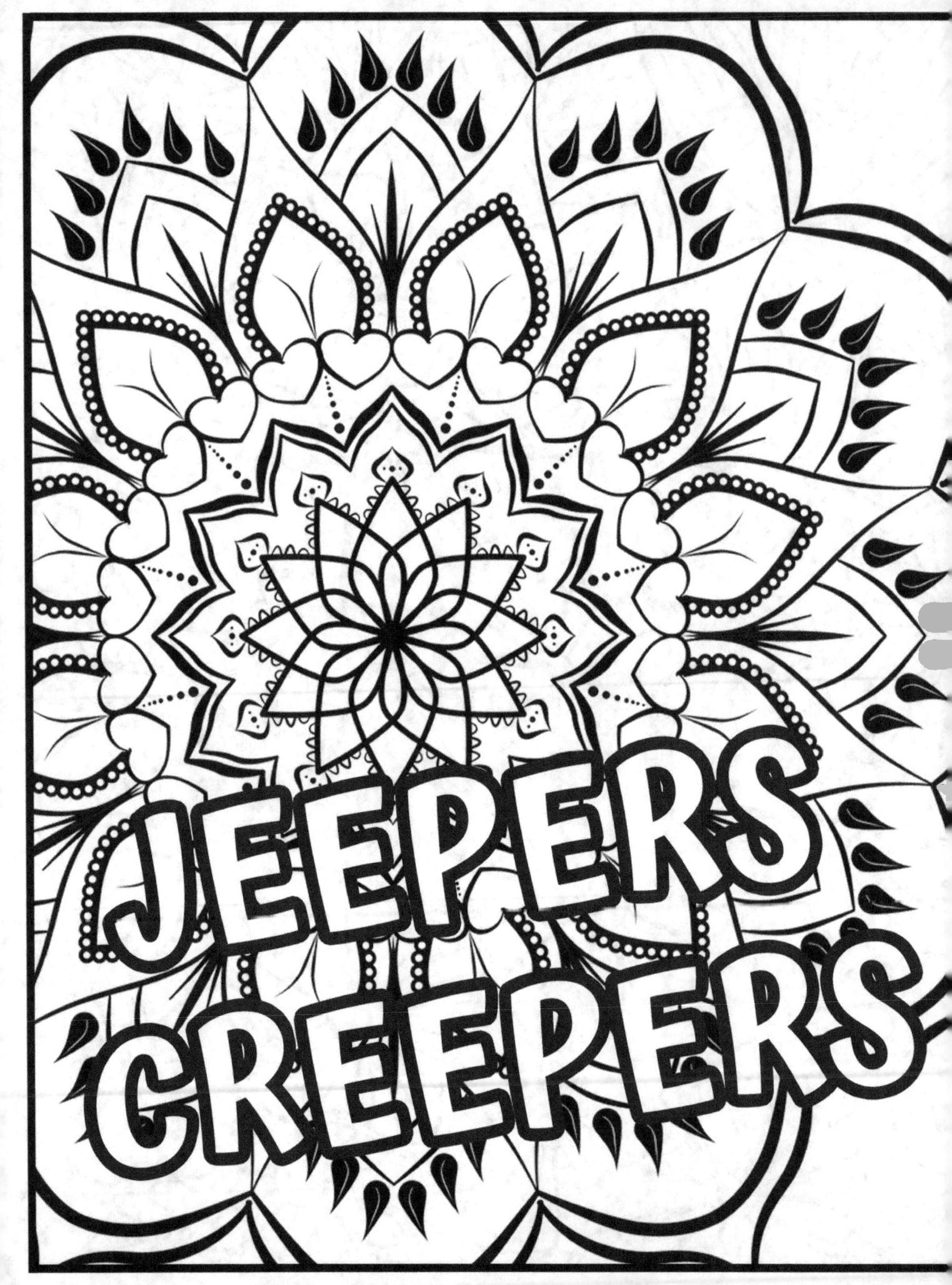

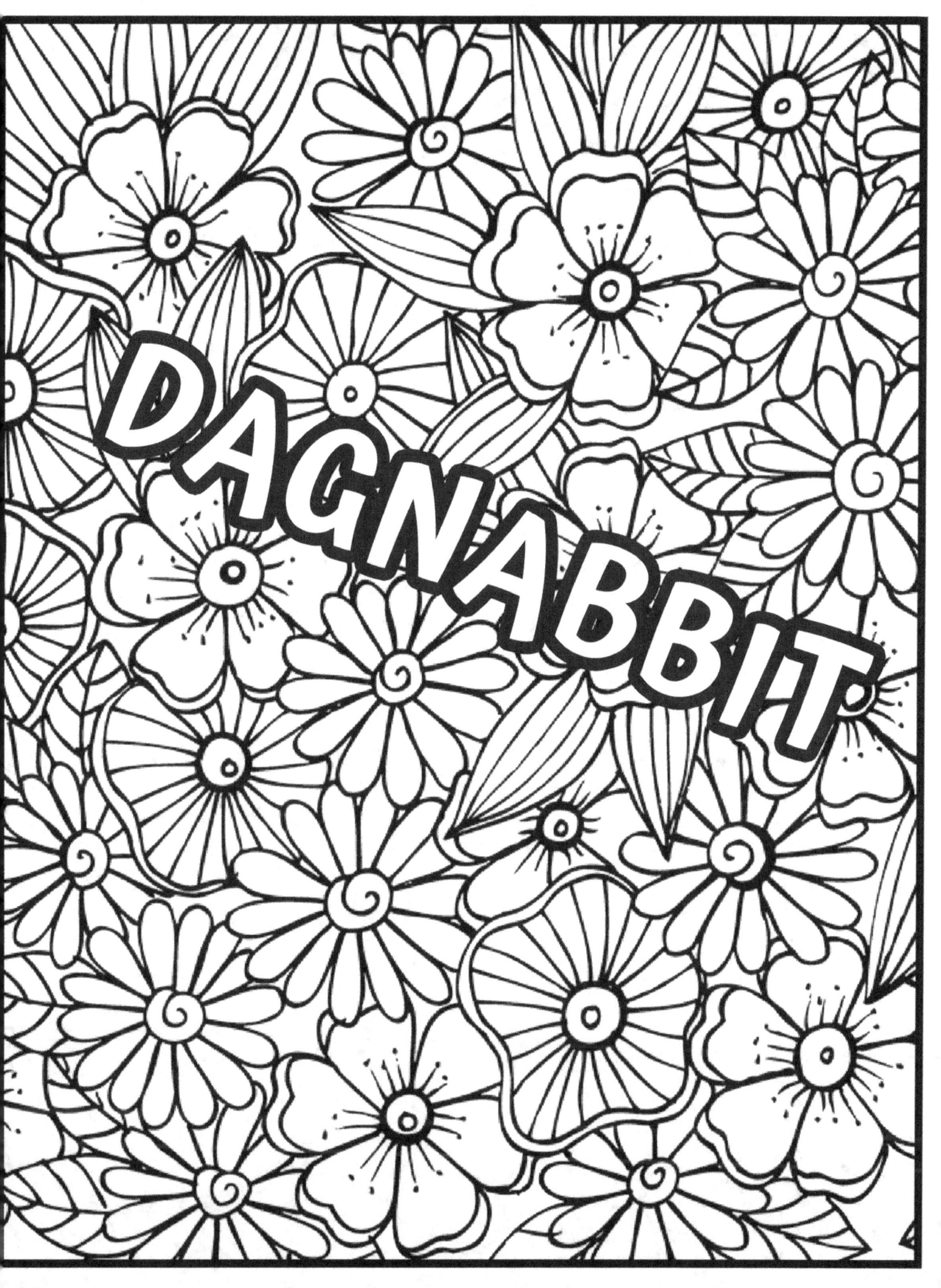

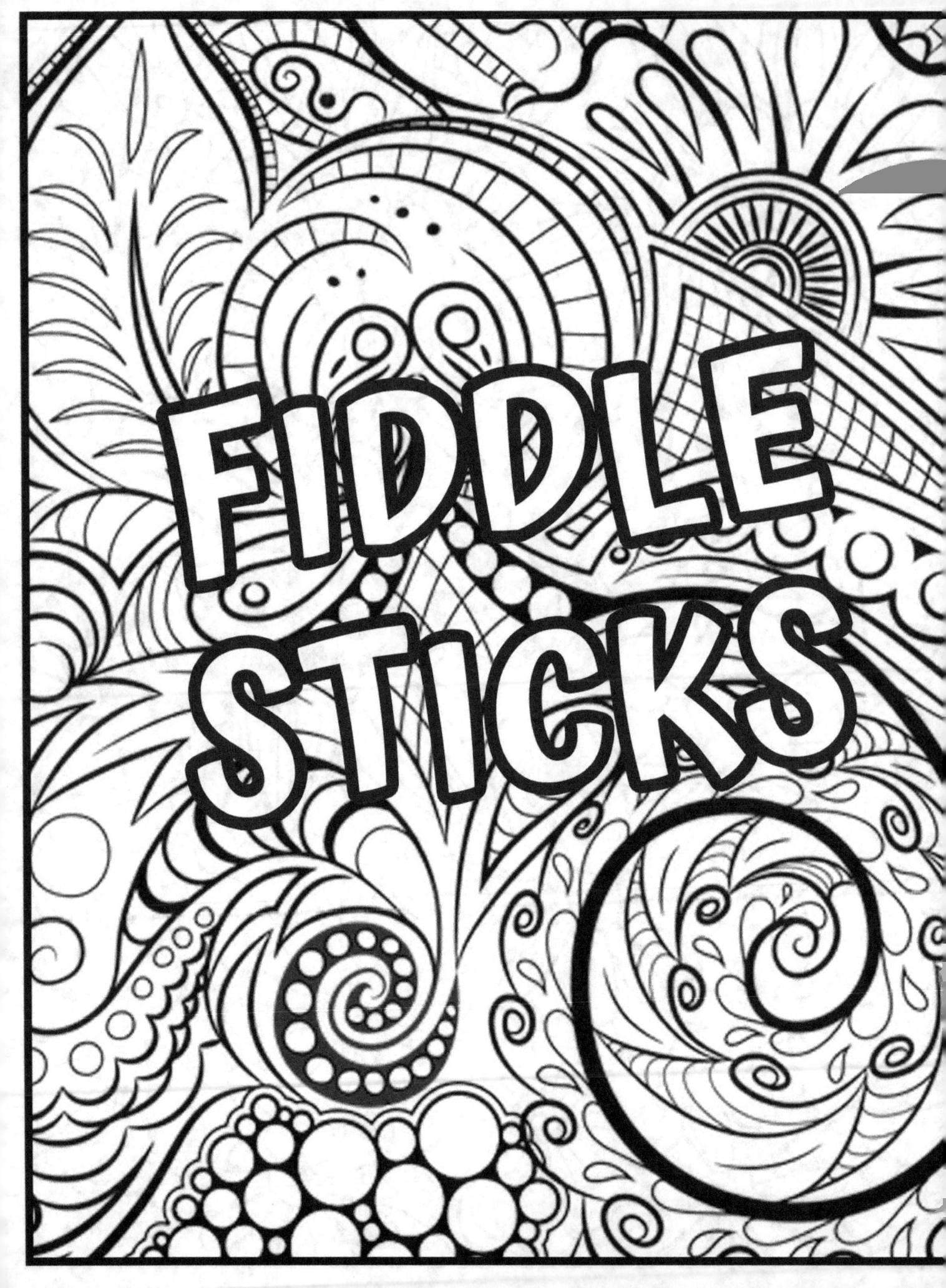

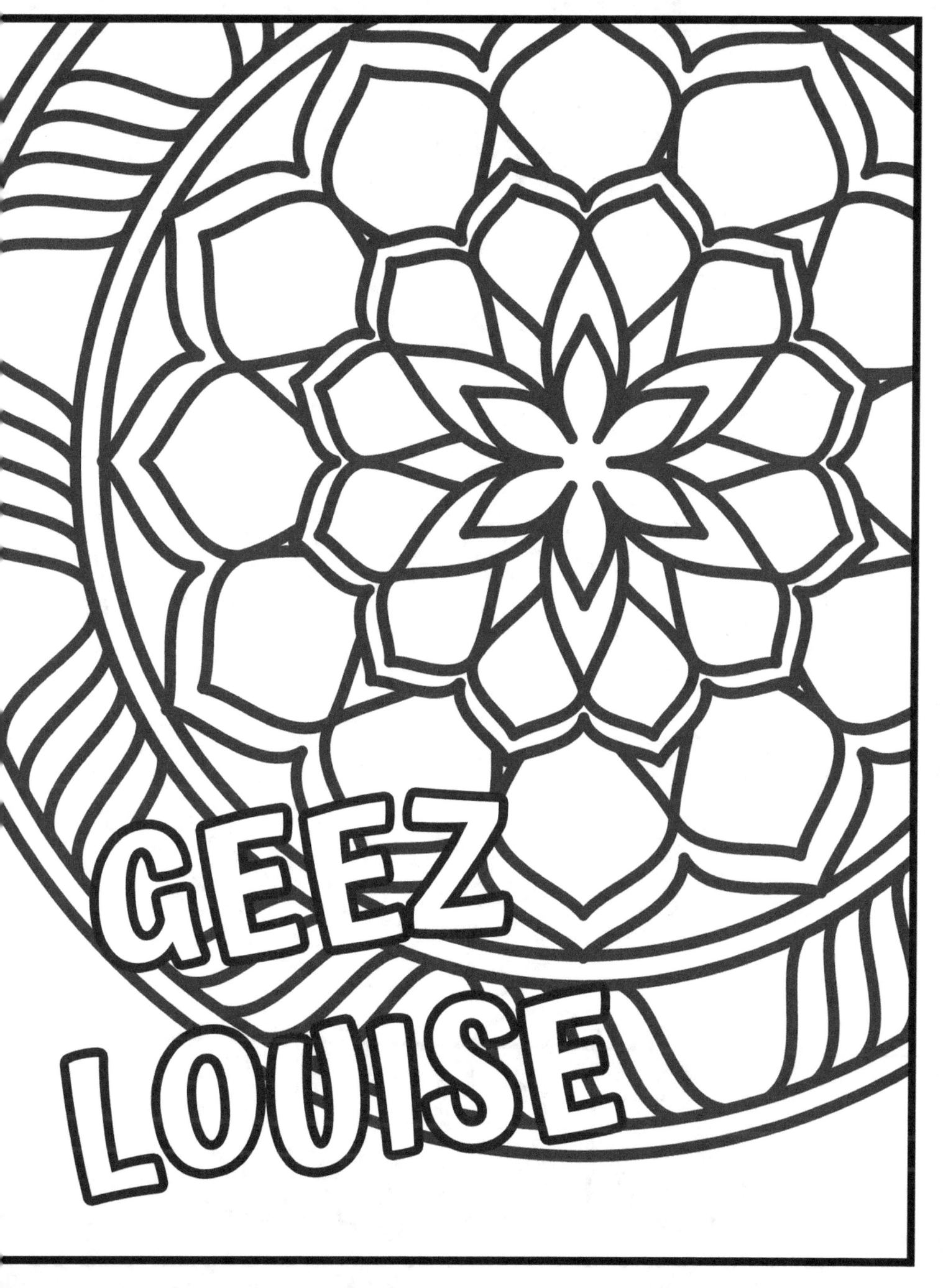

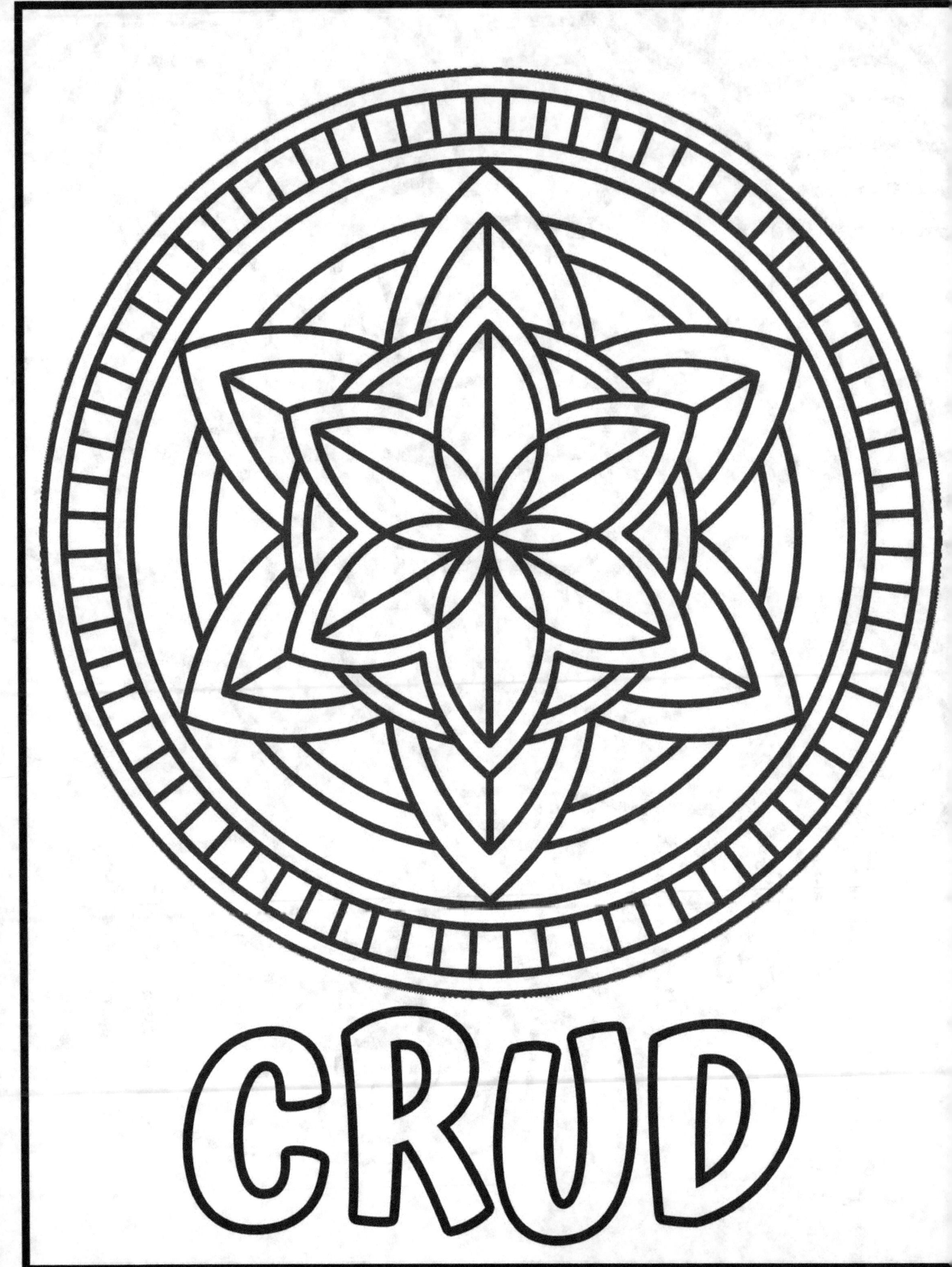

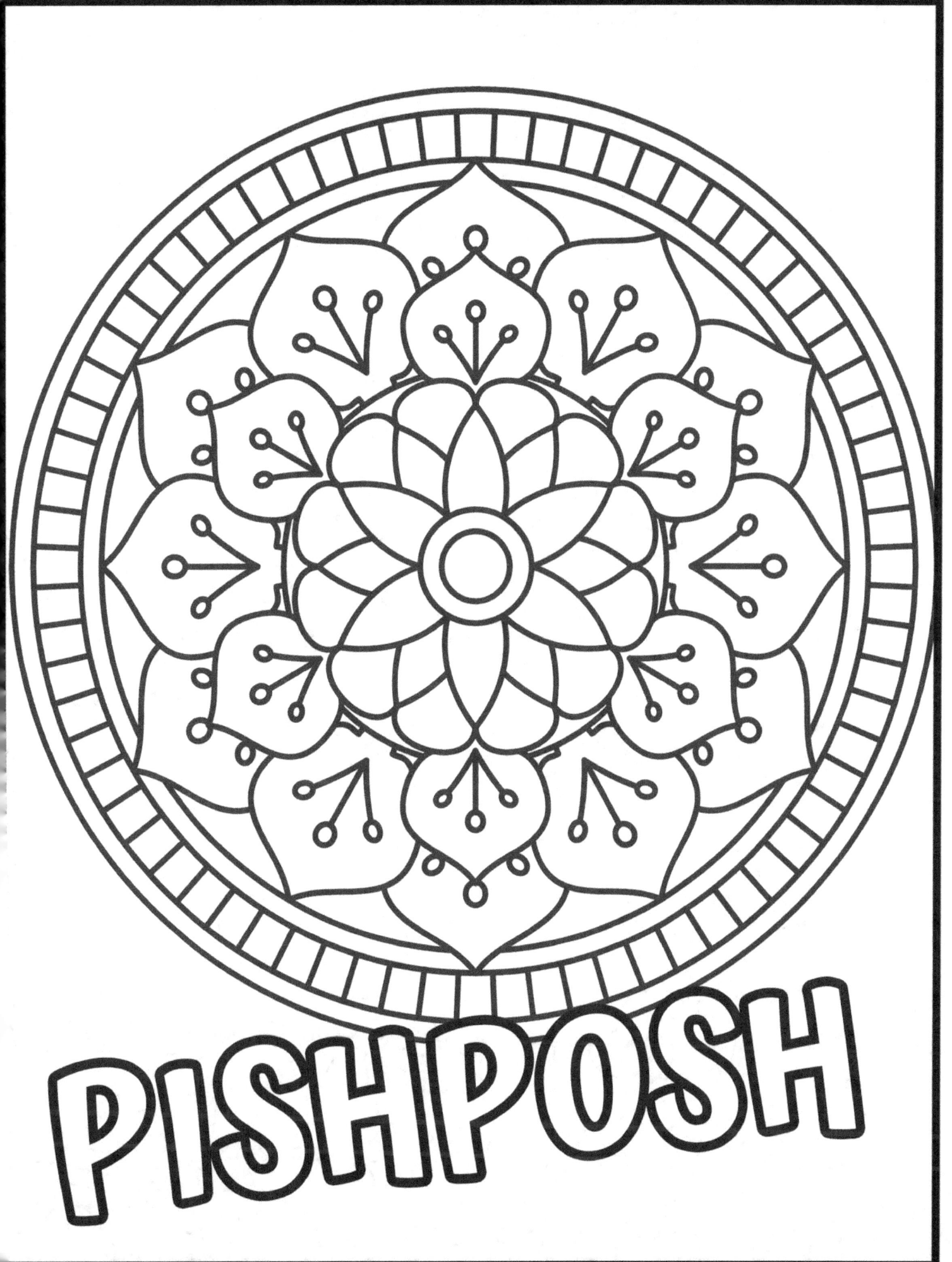

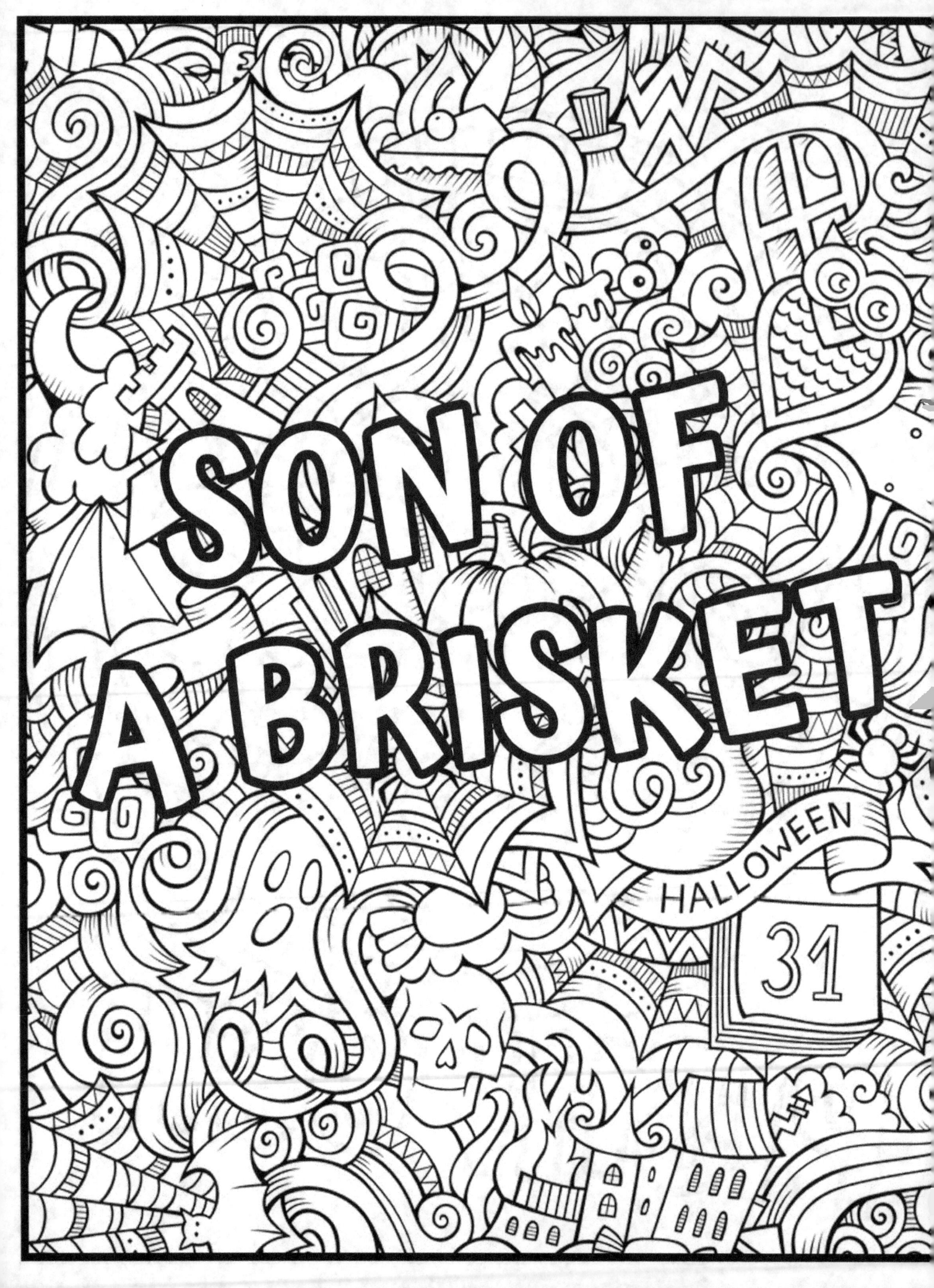

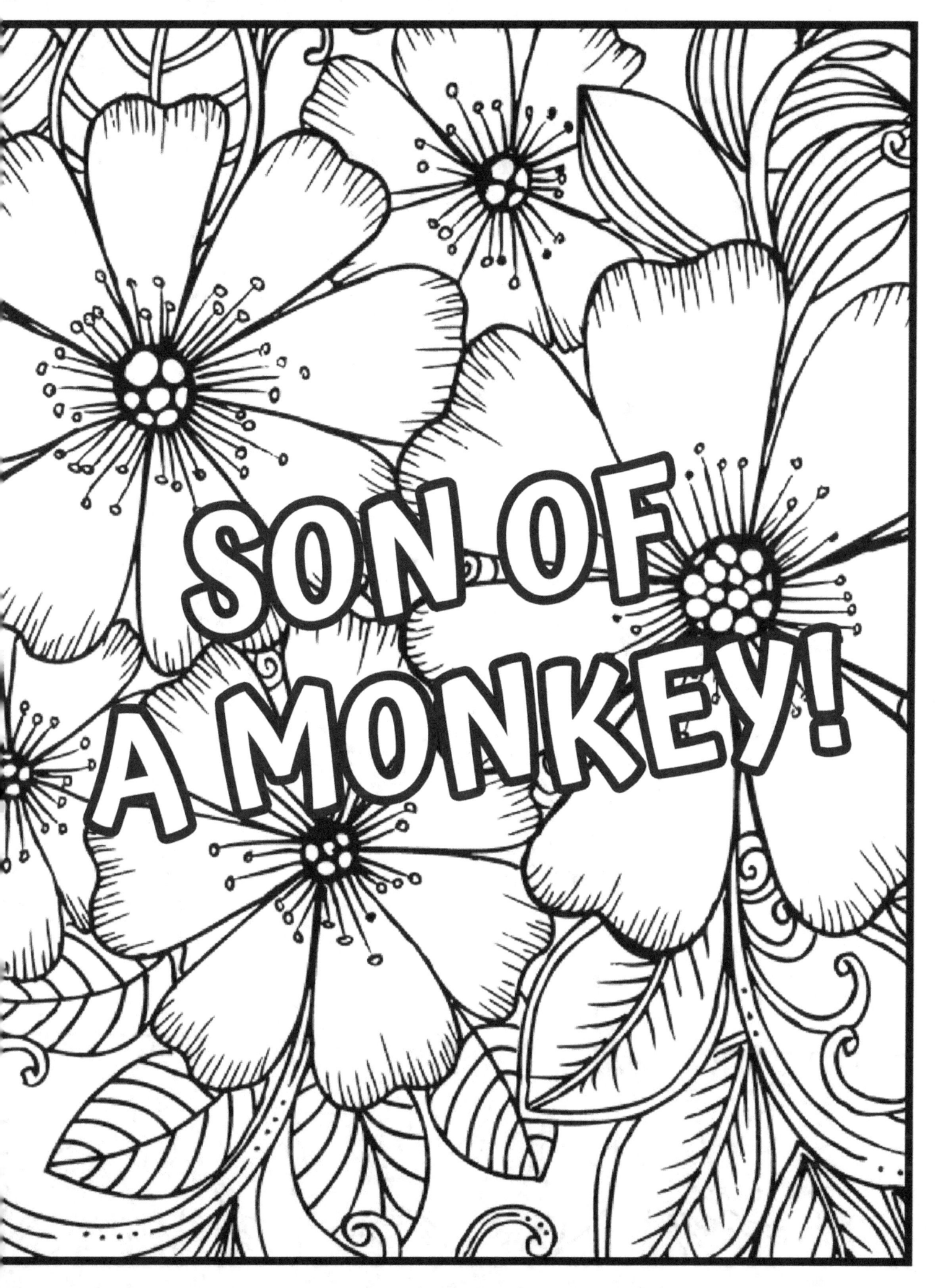

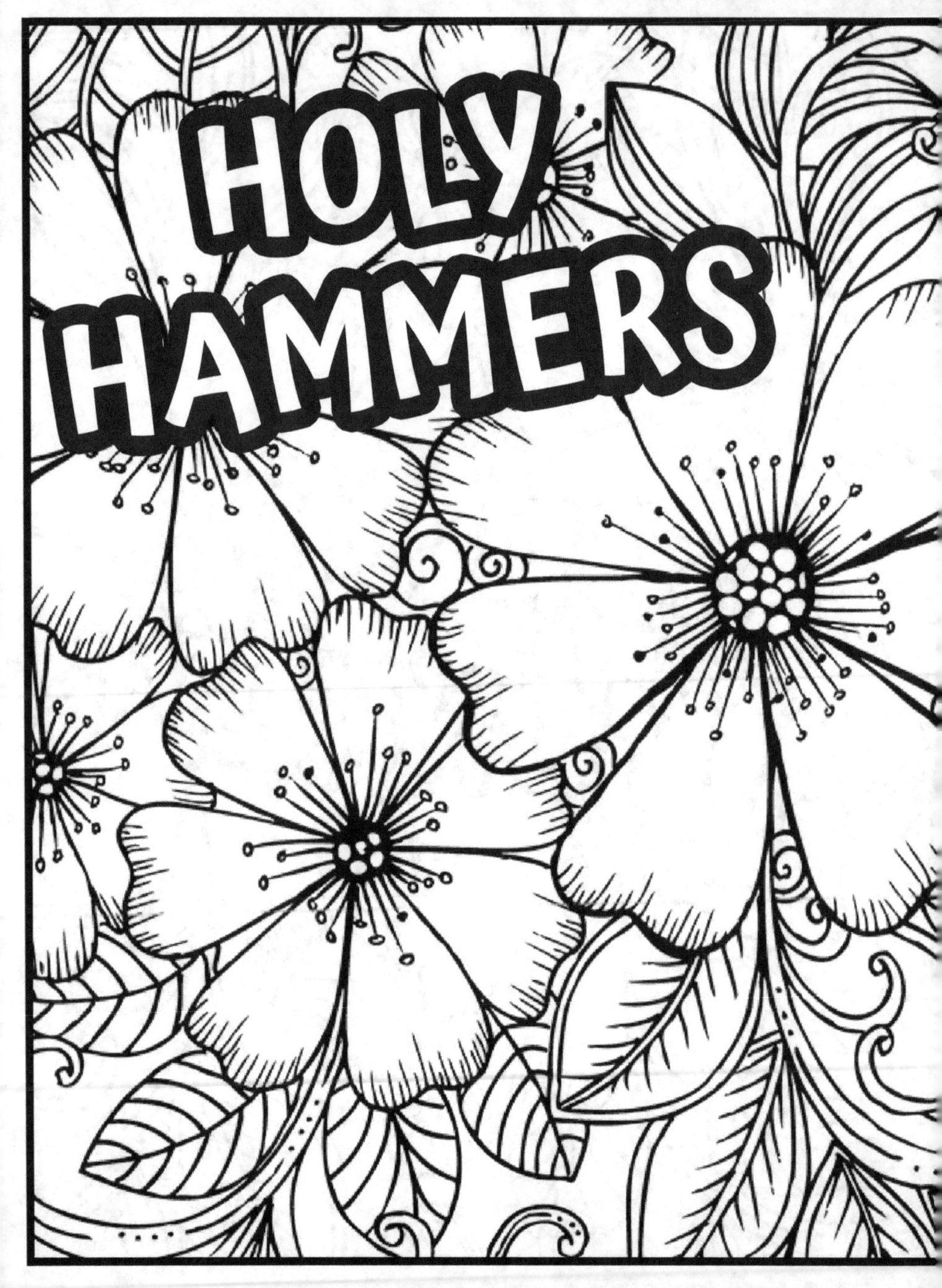

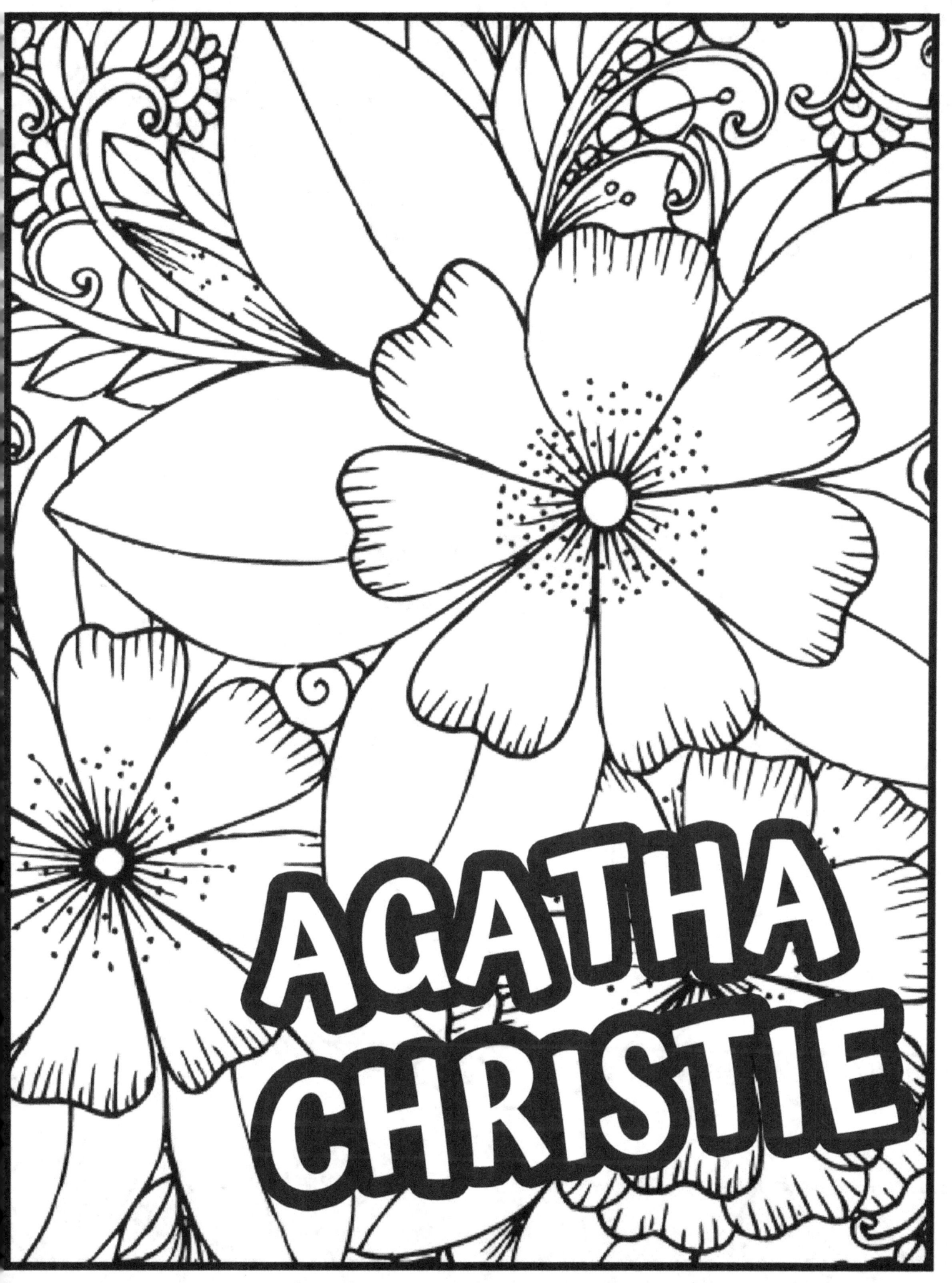

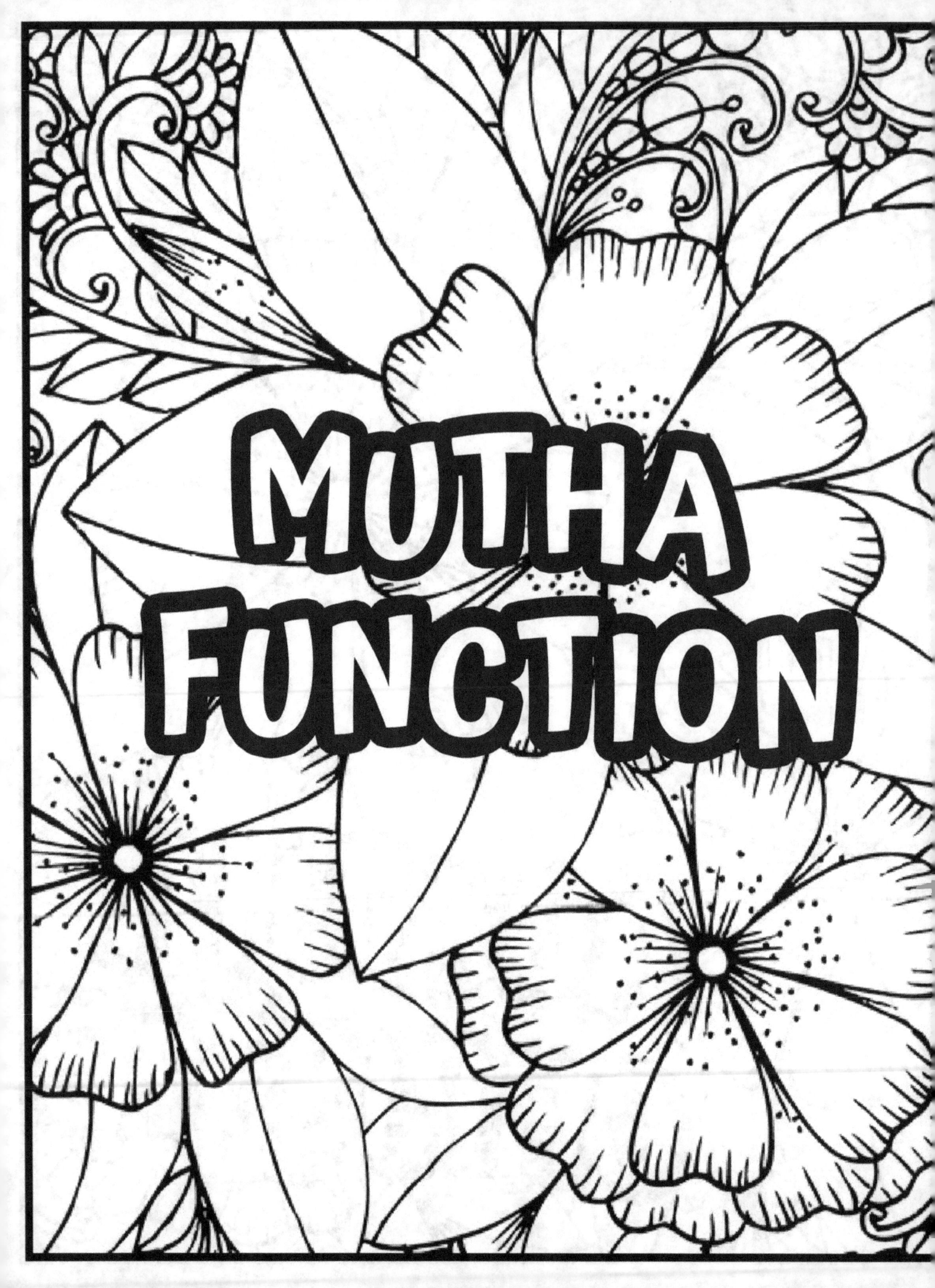

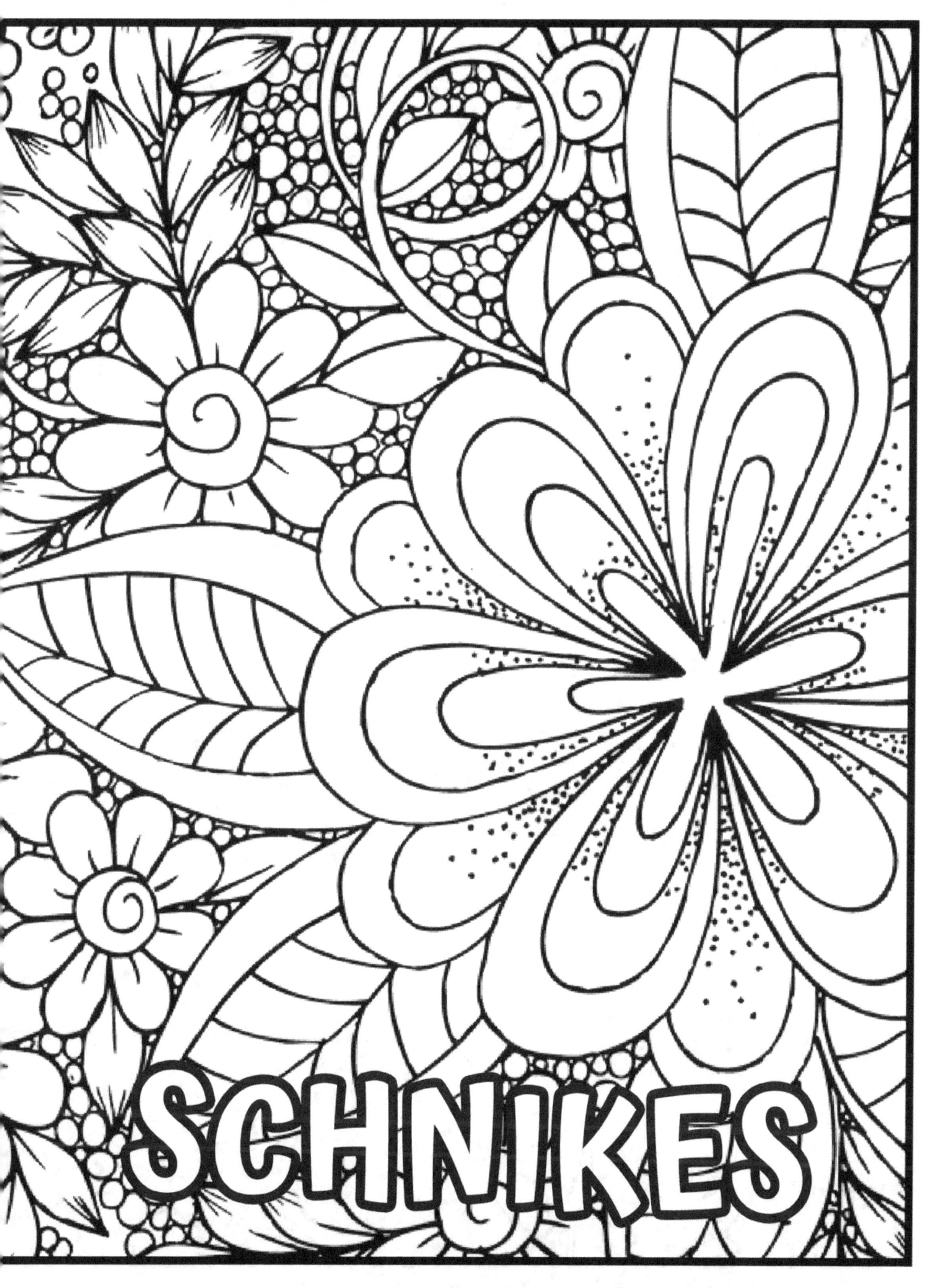

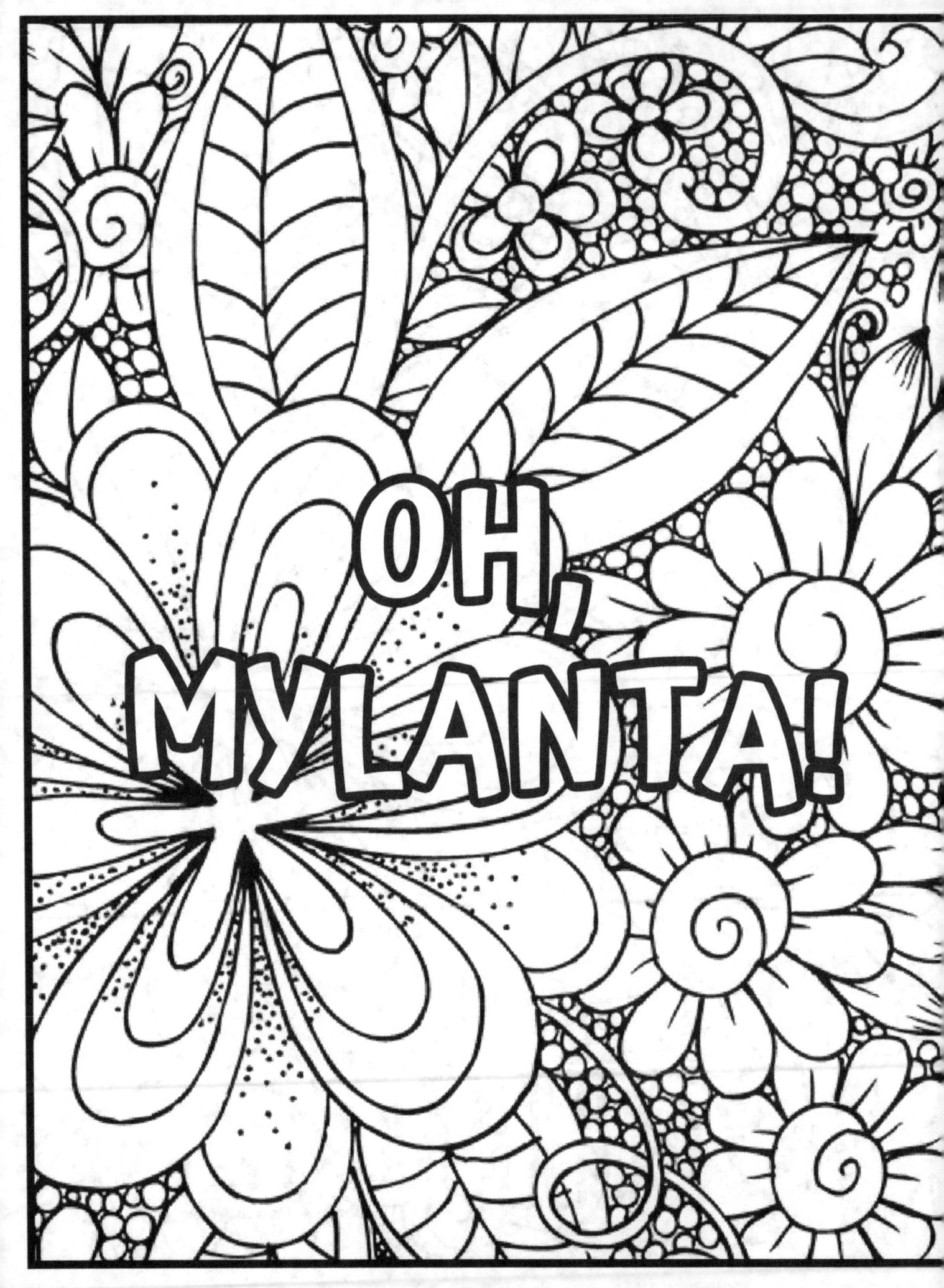

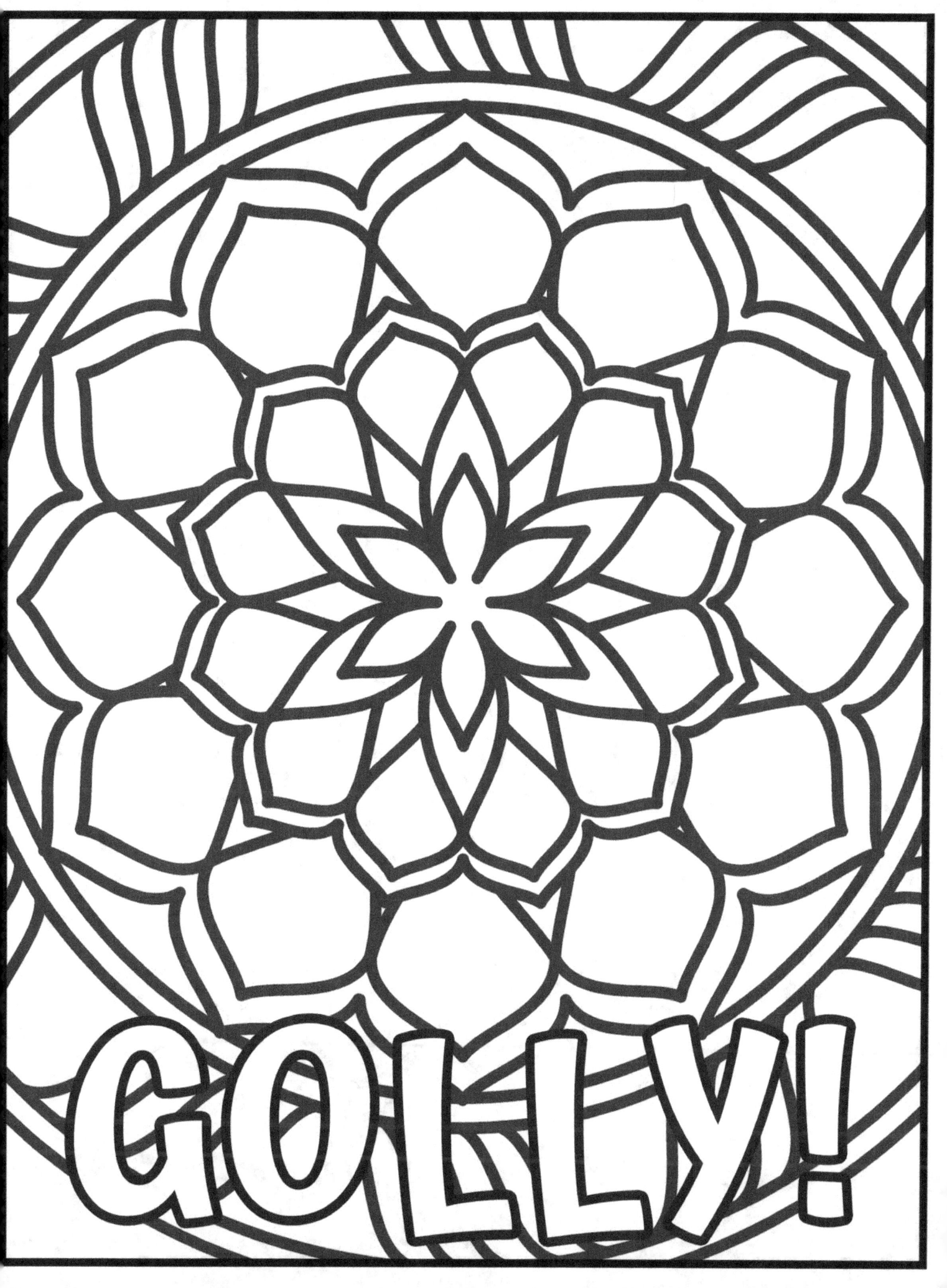

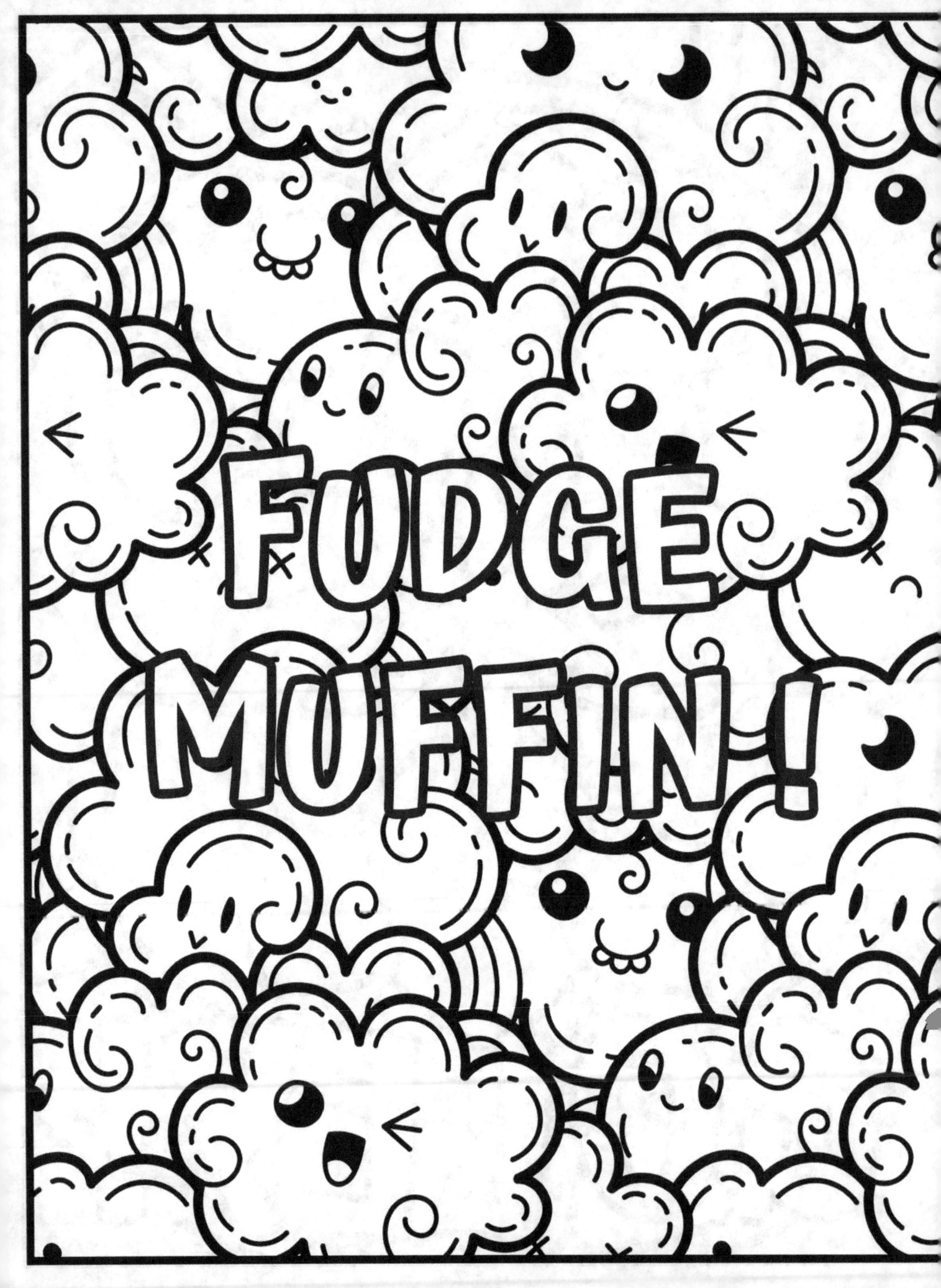

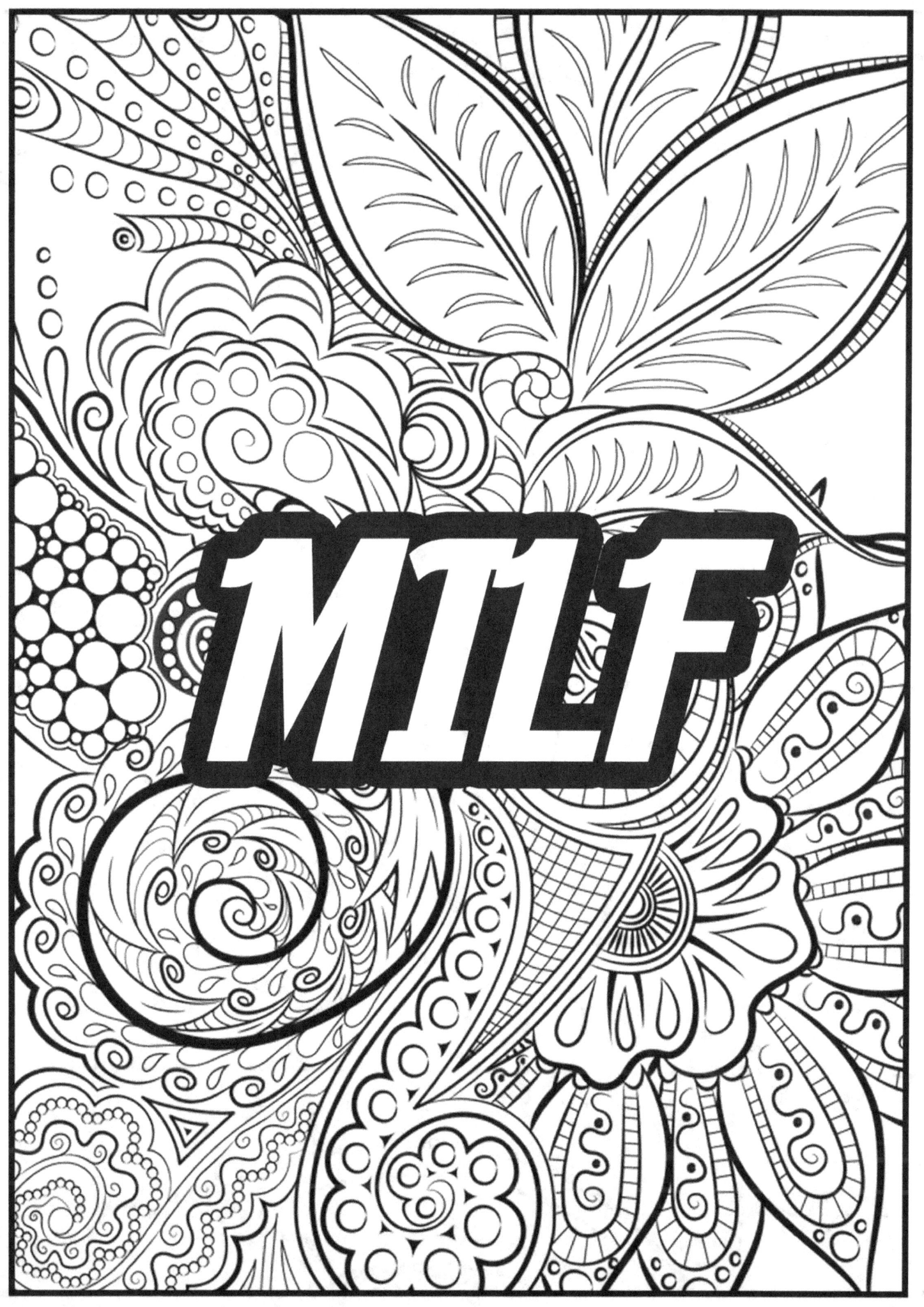

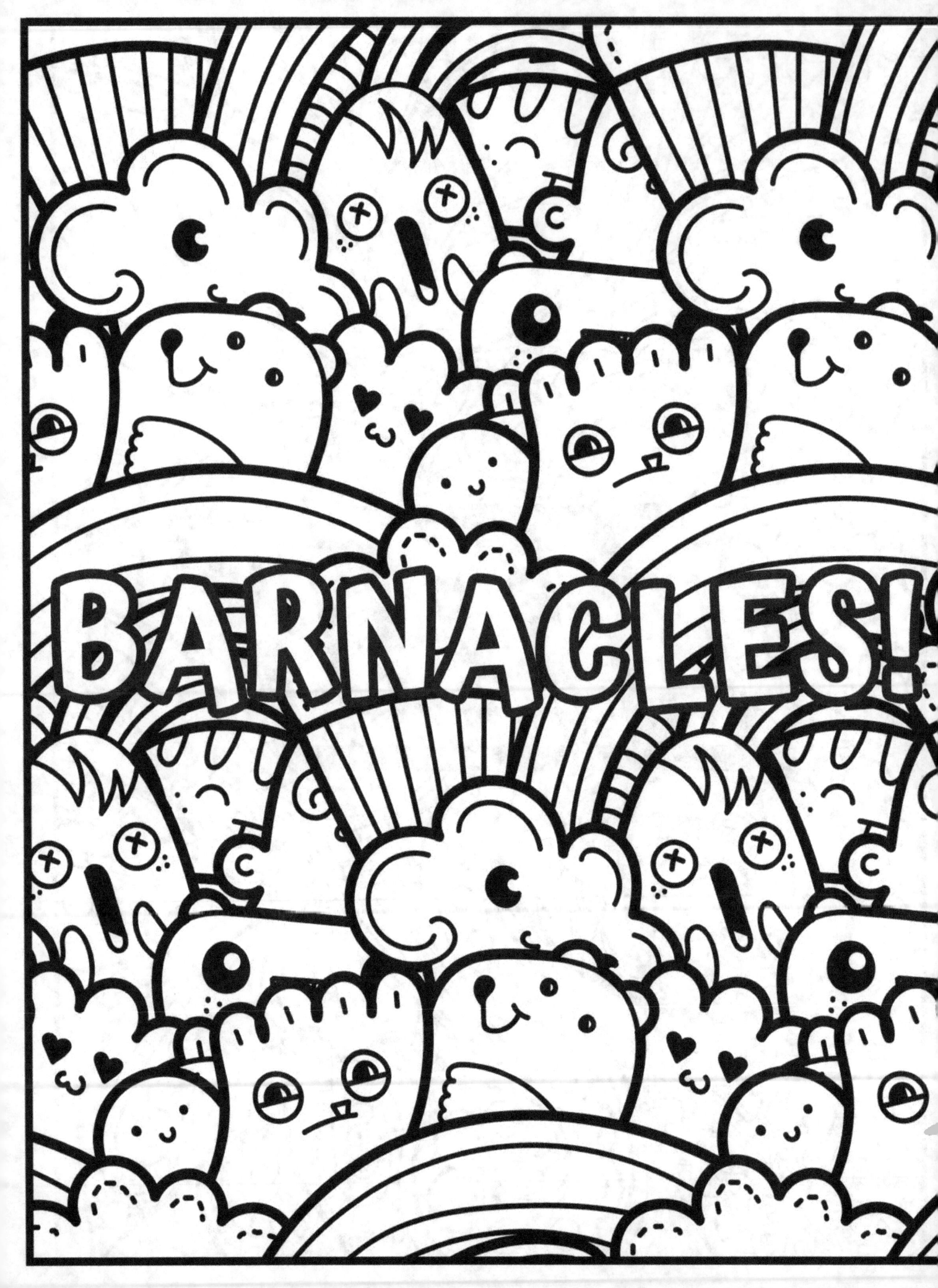

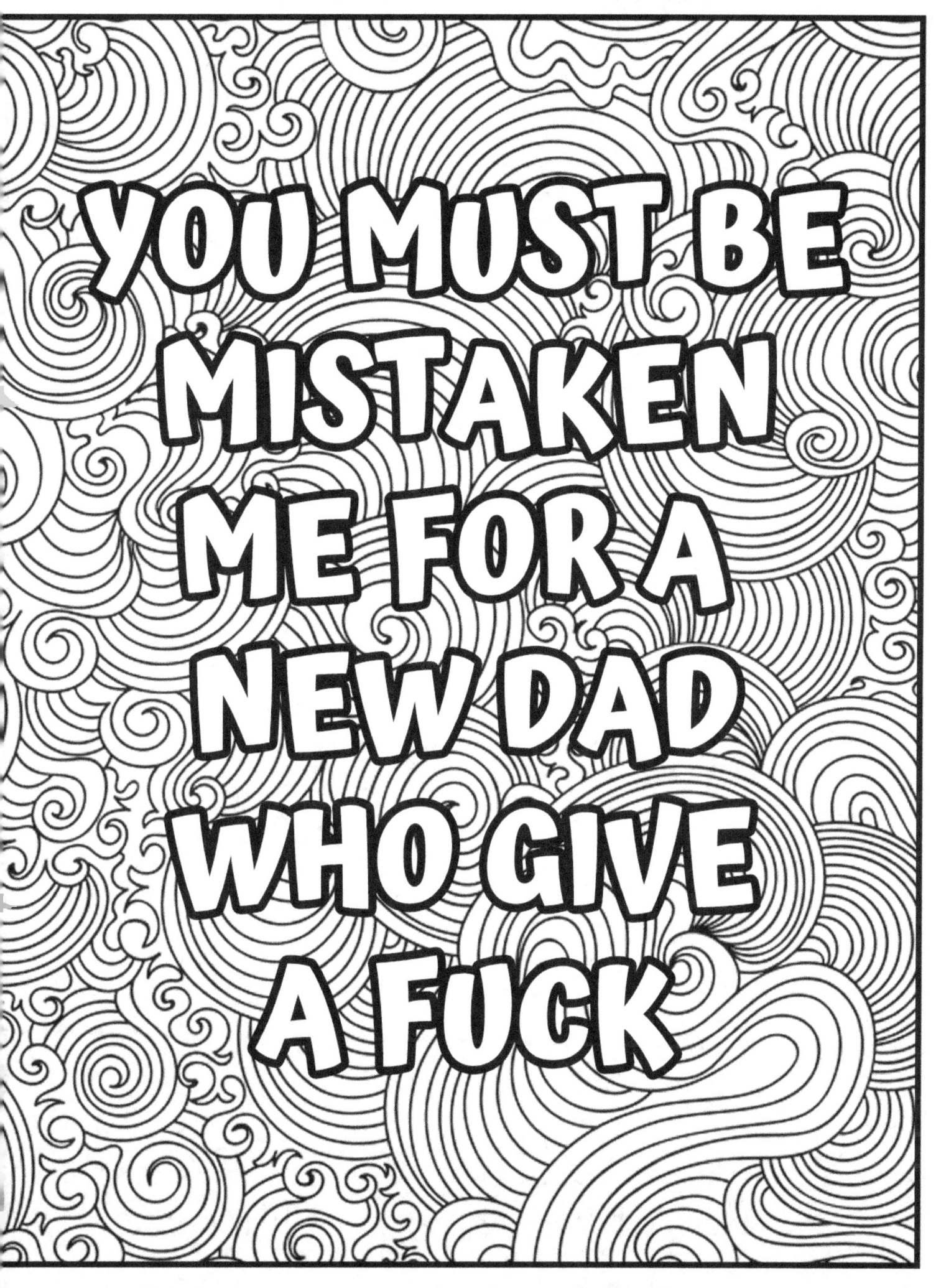

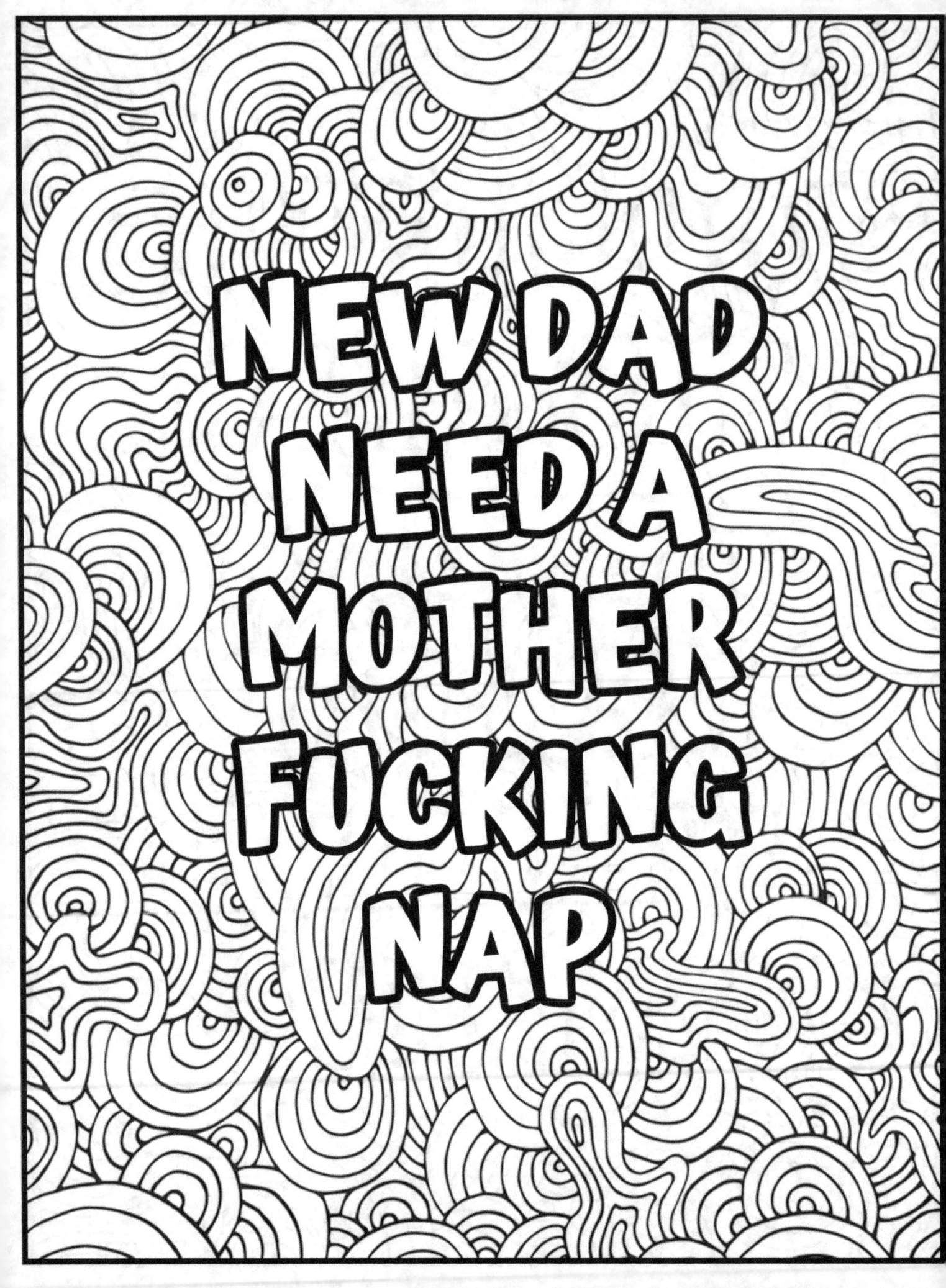

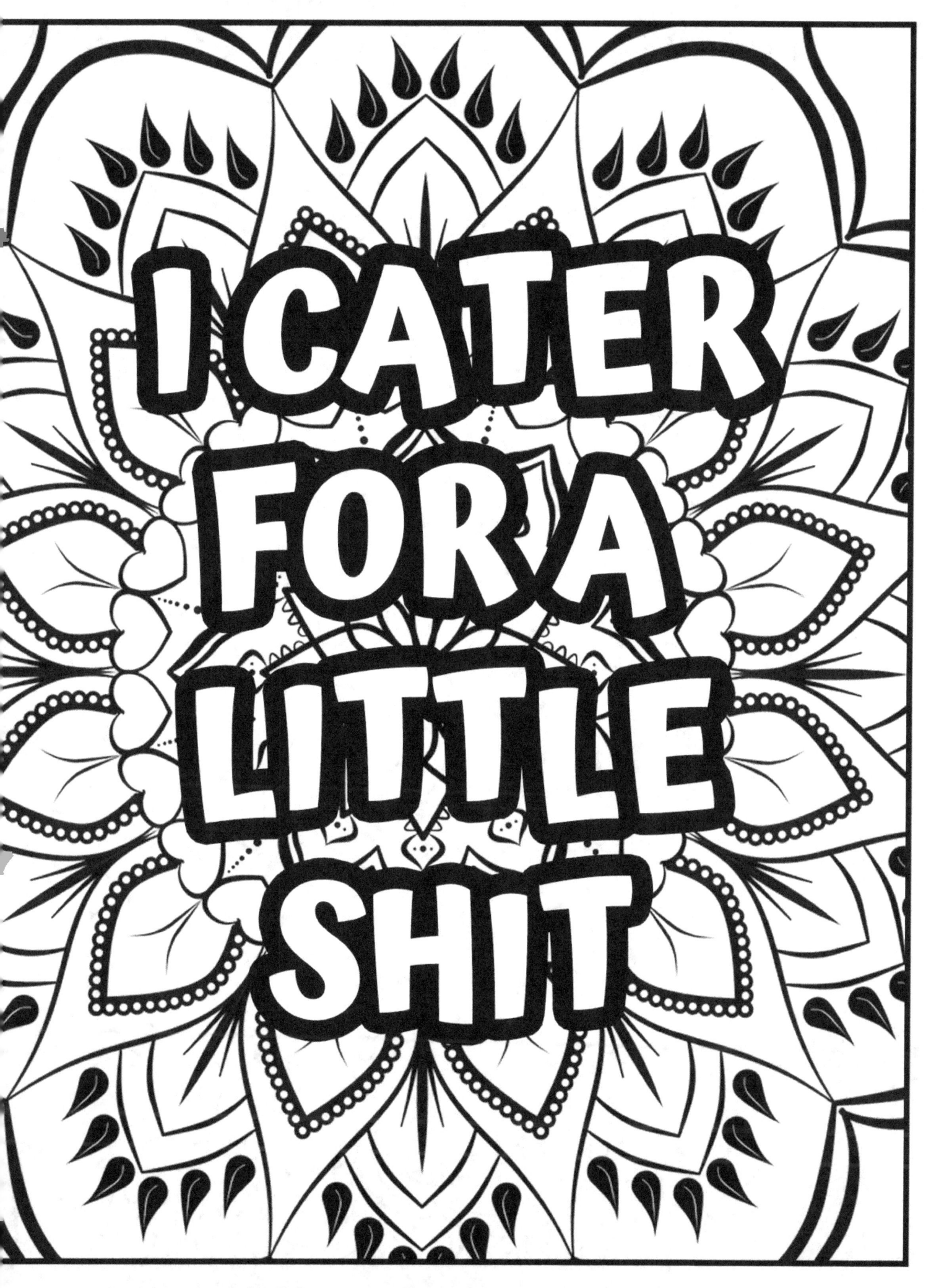

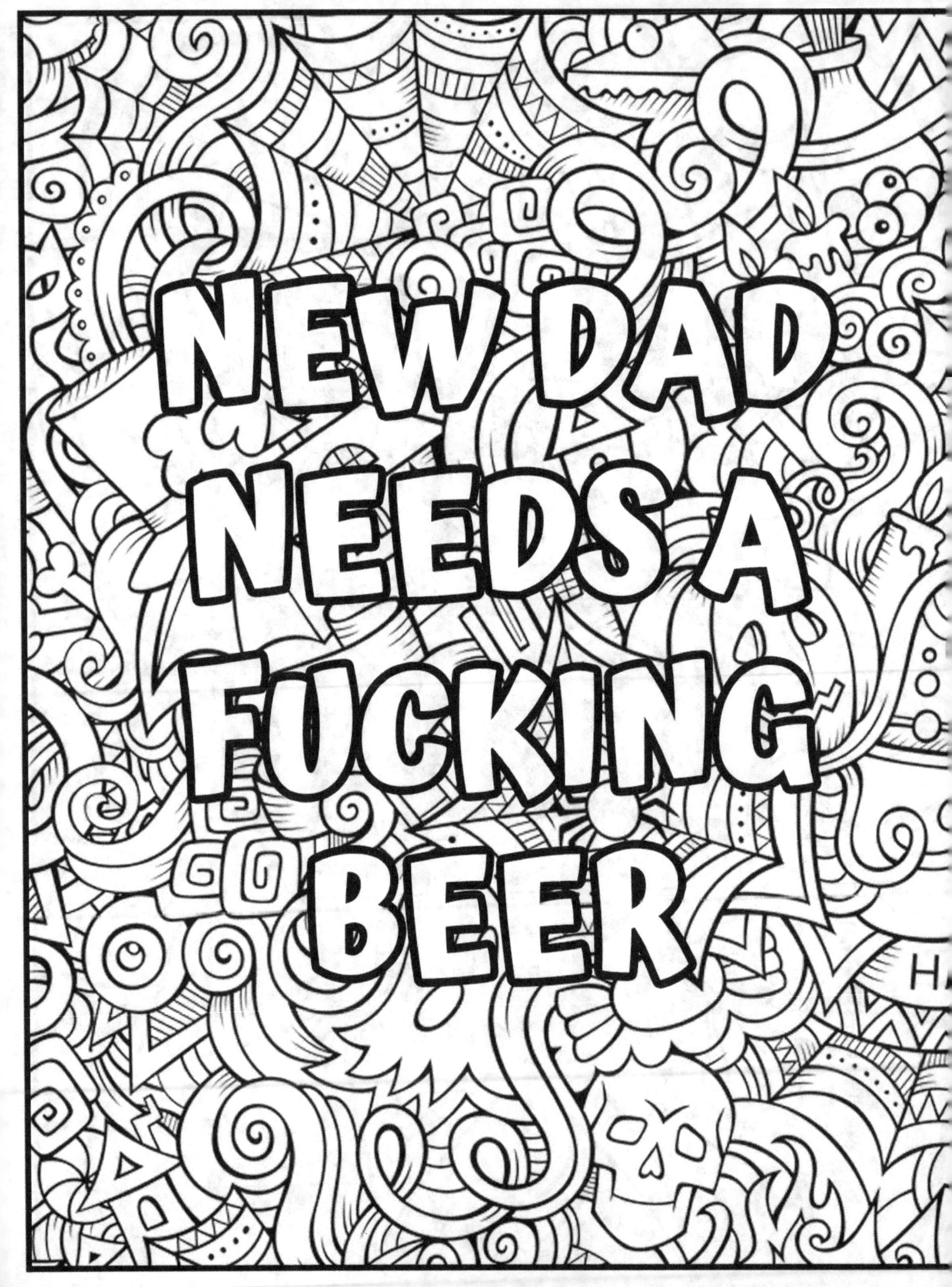

Thank you!

We hope you enjoyed our book!

As a small family company,your feedback is very important to us.

Please let us know what you think about our book at:

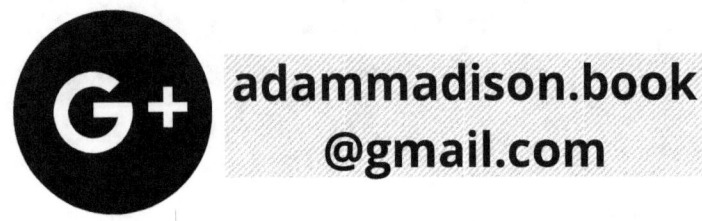 adammadison.book
@gmail.com

www.ingramcontent.com/pod-product-compliance
Lightning Source LLC
Chambersburg PA
CBHW080853220526
45467CB00008B/2487